PRAISE FOR

The Generous One

"A riveting, soul shaking, heart awakening, shivering and magnificent account of one man's wake up call – which triggers an awakening in all who read it. A profound book."

Dr. Joe Vitale,
author of *The Attractor Factor* and many more

"*Generous One* approaches the near death experience differently than the many NDE books I have read. His focus on healing takes you to a powerful nearly mystical experience. His recounting of his meeting in the "Presence" is a release of spiritual power. It brought me to tears."

Dave Edman,
Speaker and Spiritual Advisor

"Tom sent me his book the same weekend I was moving and traveling. I read one chapter and I was mesmerized. The *Generous One* holds a profound message of healing and abundance. Definitely, a must read!"

Eva Gregory,
Author of *The Feel Good Guide to Prosperity*

"Tom, I love your book. I cried, I laughed and smiled. This month there have been several family health challenges including heart surgery and dialysis. I have been doing the Arc of Light without anyone knowing I am doing it. It gives me hope when I hear them say things are better, or improving or a friend who seems to have had stress lifted off her shoulders. There is such power in this beautiful gift you have brought to the world, simple yet incredible. I read from the Generous One everyday. Bless you!"

Catherine Foster
Professional Mixed Media Artist

"We lost our son thirteen years ago, and of course, we are grieving still. When Jillian shared Tom's story my spirit lightened. I couldn't wait to read it. I think this book can be a great comfort to anyone dealing with the death of a loved one."

Ann Nava, Admin for Graphic Design Firm

"I have to tell you the Generous One is a totally riveting read! One of the most spiritually engaging accounts of an afterlife experience I've read. I have read so many of them over the years. I love the way it's written. It flows with rich imagery. Once I started reading I couldn't put it down. I love the way you refer to the Generous One. It's brilliant. You have another hit book. Congratulations, Tom."

Dr. Symeon Rodger,
Tactical and Strategic Leadership Training

...in the Presence of the
Generous One

The Miracle Healing
You Created

*For Cherie from Jill
1/1/2020*

THOMAS L. PAULEY

Rich Dreams Publishing

RICH DREAMS PUBLISHING
Published by Rich Dreams Publishing
1901 Bush Street, Number 105, Oceanside, California 92058

https://www.RichDreams.com

… in the Presence of the Generous One.
The Miracle Healing You Created

Editor: Jillian Coleman Wheeler
Cover Design: George Capielo
Cover Image, Orion Falls, used with permission Zhuoqun Wu, Chilescope 2

Special Acknowledgements

This book would not have been possible without my daughter and creative partner, Penelope J. Pauley. Her persistent demands that I wake up and write this book, and the inspired direction and the transcendent guidance and clarification she offered were invaluable. She refused a writing credit. She said, "It's your story, Dad. You don't need my name on it." She was right, of course. It is my story.

For all my daughter's brilliant contributions I offer my heartfelt gratitude.

Thank you, Penelope.

. . . . . .

It was Jillian Coleman Wheeler who took it upon herself to see to it this work became the basis for *Generous One: A Transcendent Course of Action* as well as the book you now read. I am deeply grateful for Jillian's lifelong friendship, brilliant mind, and loving insistence Generous One must become a book for all to read.

Thank you. Thank you. Thank you, Jillian.

. . . . . .

As valuable as a divinely inspired idea or good writing is there is something even more important – bringing your efforts to a conclusion. Through it all Diane was there with me. She always had my back whispering words of encouragement, loving me when I didn't love myself and kicking my backside when I needed that. I wouldn't have come close to finishing Generous One without her. I am honored to thank my wife, lover and partner of fifty-one years and counting, Diane Renee Pauley.

For this and all the wonderful adventures and impossible dreams we continue to live.

Thank you, Diane.

. . . . . .

Many friends and family have freely given me their unwavering support, helping me bring my efforts to a successful conclusion. Jillian, of course, separated the spiritual from the mundane in critical times, helping me see the forest when I was fixated on the heavenly trees. From the beginning, she believed in this book, and went above and beyond the bonds of friendship. My other brother, Dempsey, was the king of stability and forbearance through his own difficulties. Lisa and Bob held tight to our love, always abundant with generosity, becoming my rock of strength in the good times and the rough times. Barbara and Dean, close family through shared battles, were a constant reminder that a good ole Nebraska boy could always get 'er done. David was always available, my go to source for spiritual confirmation and deep conversation. Lynn kept me home writing when distraction threatened my continuance. My dear daughter, Heather, kicked open the locked and sealed door to my continued healing and recovery. My brother, Mark, stepped in as the perfect battlefield engineer, constantly building bridges and helping me eliminate my many defects. Through it all, my son-in-law, Chris, maintained my hopes and dreams with his calm demeanor and attention to detail. My son, Alex, was perhaps the greatest inspiration of all, lending his support at a moment's notice selflessly and without fail. I watched him become the man I always knew he was. I am overwhelmed by their support and love. They helped me gain a new perspective on my human family. And when our journey hit rough seas Cheri and Doug were ready with a port in the storm.

God bless y'all.

Dedication

During the holiday season a few years ago, Diane and I attended a wedding of friends at the Coronado Hotel in San Diego. I had given one impromptu lecture in another friend's "Faire Garden" that summer. I'd mentioned the possibility of writing this book. I had no more than sat down at the wedding celebration when a friend who had attended that lecture came up to me and asked about the book. I told him I hadn't started it yet and wasn't sure I would. He said, "Oh, I sure hope you do write that book. I know it would be a great benefit to all the men and women coming home from the war. That new armor protects their vital organs, but they sacrifice their arms and legs. I volunteer at the VA and I know your book would be an inspiration to their recovery."

His comments gave me the emotional push I needed to begin.

• • • • • •

I dedicate this book to all the veterans of war who have suffered mental, emotional, physical and psychological trauma and now face the lonely and difficult path of recovery.

God bless you and thank you for all you have given.

Table of Contents

How Your Miracle Healing Works

All Healing Begins With A Desire To Heal

Becoming A Quantum Magnet For Infinite Abundance

The Miracle
Healing
You Created

CHAPTER 1
The Mystery Begins

On March 28, 2009 I died.

I did return to life, but I was permanently paralyzed on the right side of my body. I was unable to sit up, eat, speak, or even comprehend where I was or what had happened to me.

The prognosis was a massive stroke directly on the brainstem requiring lifelong bed care. I heard this second hand from my wife, Diane, and daughter, Penelope, much later. I was not available at the time. The doctors offered them no hope of my recovery or improvement.

Early the following morning, March 29th, I died a second time from another stroke. Nobody had to tell me I died; that part was self-evident. I returned a second time. This time I came back with the promise of a full and complete recovery. I could talk, pull myself up, eat and comprehend my situation. Best of all, the dead area in my brain was no longer on my brain stem. It had moved.

The dead spot moved! Mysteriously, inexplicably, a dead spot the size of a racquetball in my brain seemed to have moved.

How was that possible? I was permanently bedridden only hours earlier. How could my second death improve my condition? Did the doctors misdiagnose me or give me some wonder drug? Was my improved condition the result of divine blessing? A miracle from God?

Or was it something more arcane? More esoteric? Something perhaps generated and better understood through the quantum perspective of the 21st century? Something from which all humankind could profit? Especially those reading this book.

The message and the gift I bear can improve your life beyond all human expectations. It contains a power that can change hearts and move mountains. You already have the essence of that power within you – that Miracle Healing power. I know because I watched you use it in my moment of need. Yes, you, the one reading about all this for the very first time. I saw you use the power described in this book in my greatest moment of need.

This wouldn't be a mystery if everything were simple and apparent, right?

Why did I choose to come back? Yes, it was a choice. What did I gain from coming back? What will you gain from my return? And, most importantly, what can you gain only from my gift and my experience? All these are important questions answered in this book.

What really happened in those brief moments beyond the bounds of our temporal human experience was a miracle, a miracle you created, my blessed friends.

This book can help you reunite with the Miracle Healing you sent me during my second death experience back on March 29, 2009. Oh, yes! You did send a Miracle Healing to me back then, let there be no mistake about it. Why don't you remember it? Because I haven't shown you how to do it, yet. That's right. First, I have to show you how to send a Miracle Healing back in time and into another dimension. Then, of course, you will have sent it.

Please, stay with me. I know what I'm saying seems a little odd right now. I guarantee you won't feel that way by the end of this book. Besides, it's too soon to focus on the time-space continuum, time travel or the inner workings of our temporal matrix, for that matter. Just remember my favorite line from the movie, *Fifth Element*. It seems to sum up the whole mystery.

"Time is not important; only life is important."

This is a Miracle Healing you will send, and which I know you can send because you have already sent it. I wouldn't be writing this book if you hadn't. You do this because it guarantees you and all those you love a healing that is so powerful and so advanced it is beyond all current human comprehension.

This book holds a gift for all humankind I brought back from the Presence of the Generous One. You have been expecting this book for a very long time. You asked me to bring it back to remind you exactly how powerful, how truly elevated and mindful you really are. It is a divine talisman, so timely and so earth shockingly important it can and will affect your life, my life and the lives of those you love for centuries to come.

To better understand this opportunity and the magnitude of your miracle healing powers, we will begin by identifying the major problem limiting your health, wealth and happiness today.

First, however, we must make a quick stop on the way. It will be quick, I promise. It always is.

Healing Is
The Essential
Lodestone Of
All Abundance

CHAPTER 2

Code Blue

As I lay flat on my back in the Emergency Room of Saddleback Hospital surrounded by my kids, knowing that my wife Diane was already in the air flying home from the vacation that was not to be, I felt strangely secure. As though I'd wake at any moment and discover all this dreadful reality I was steadfastly refusing to accept was only a grim nightmare, God's way of getting my attention, warning me to change my ways, or perhaps opening the door to some hidden opportunity, or maybe some good material for another book.

I couldn't be having a stroke. Not me, Mr. Positive, Mr. Green-Drinks-Once-A-Day, Mr. Mind-Over-Matter. Not Tom Pauley. My brain couldn't be dying. Not my precious brain. The concept was just too gruesome to consider. It simply wasn't possible. No, I couldn't be having a stroke.

Actually, I'd already had five. They were mild. The doctors – there were a lot of them – told me the four I had in the Emergency Room were aftershocks or stutters to the first one, the TIA, that so rudely interrupted my life and brought me here in the first place. But I shouldn't worry. All five were rather mild as strokes go.

Unfortunately, two more strokes were coming. And they weren't going to be stutters. They were the main attraction. The ones you don't come back from. Pulse stoppers. Widow makers. Stone cold killers.

The Shot

Of course, I didn't know that then. I was still joking and laughing with my kids. Feeling bad that Diane had cut her trip short for nothing. After all, the head nurse had just told me there would be no more hurried trips down that long corridor to the little room where they took pictures of my brain. The doctors were confident that the culprit was an obstruction of a blood vessel supplying blood to the brain, an ischemic stroke. Since I wasn't having ruptured blood vessels, a hemorrhagic stroke, they could finally give me the "The Shot" that would speed my recovery. The magic shot they can only give you within two hours of an ischemic stroke, the shot that cost nearly a year's salary all by itself. And which they seemed reluctant to administer at all.

Because as I found out later, it was a tad bit experimental. Guinea pig or not, I readily agreed.

Thank God, we'd been able to afford health insurance finally after forty years of marriage, because once you land in a hospital they want an insurance card that guarantees they'll get paid, or buckets of cash. No matter how much money you have, it's never enough. Dying is a very expensive business these days. Then, however, money was the last thing on my mind.

I had always taken good health for granted. I felt like I was indestructible. Sure, I had high blood pressure and diabetes, but I just figured I ran a little hot. Irish hot. I was a tough skinned survivor from way back. Besides I was sure that what you didn't give energy to would go away. Who was I kidding? I told my wife for years we'd die in a private plane crash over the Pacific Ocean when we were 110. I don't know if she believed it, but apparently I believed it myself.

All of a sudden good health was all I could think about.

I had never considered health much of a benefit in my life. I had never really been ill before, and when we had to get into a hospital I managed to hustle my way in. I always believed I was blessed. I figured I must have a guardian angel or something sitting on my shoulder. Since childhood I was obsessed with getting rich in the most material sense of the word. I always knew I was destined to be swimming in gold, silver and diamonds. Once I hit it really big, I could have anything I wanted. Good health too, I guess.

Probably why I lived most of my life on the edge. Pushing, always pushing. Testing the limits. Knowing deep inside that I couldn't lose. That as long as I trusted in my God-given talents and abilities, which I believed were great, then I would weather any storm and cross any divide. I could do anything, go anywhere and become anyone I wanted. On top of that I was convinced that because of my Irish heritage I had been granted an inordinate degree of luck. Good luck. I felt like a modern day gunslinger roaming the Wild West in search of that big score that would once and for all set him free from the trials and tribulation of an ordinary life.

Money Is A Blinding Mistress

It didn't matter that I'd already put my family through years of rented houses, uncertainty and risk. Moving from neighborhood to neighborhood, city-to-city and state-to-state while I sought my fortune. No, that didn't matter. Because my ego only considered the one ultimate benefit as a benefit worth seeking. Success meant getting rich, and that was my destiny. Regardless of the fact I had two bankruptcies, three home foreclosures and a couple of car repossessions to my name by this time, I was on my way. In some ways I lived life as the character in the old, old song, *Roving Gambler,* by Tennessee Ernie Ford. It was one of the few records my uncle and I listened to when I was a boy, after my parents' divorce. Dumb lyrics actually, but to me those lyrics glorified a life free of outside control and manipulation. The rugged individualist. The self-reliant cowboy, who owed no one, served no one, and whose success depended solely on his confidence and his own God-given abilities.

What can I say? I was only nine. But it stuck.

So like the lyrics of that song, I was a rovin' gambler. I gambled all around. Wherever I met with a good idea I laid my money down. Even if I had to borrow some first. Oh, I eventually altered my attitude, but not until I had spent years ramming my head into that stonewall of material success at any cost. I learned how to survive. How to live on the edge. How to start from nothing over and over again. But it wasn't until I met Marilyn, the woman who inspired our first book, that I learned how to get everything I wanted in life. Without enslaving myself to the whims of the market place or the dreams of others. The secret I'd sought my whole life was so simple it boggles the mind.

Wealth is our birthright, a gift from our Creator. Bestowed upon request.

I thought I had finally made it. Nirvana. I had found the pathway to a rich and happy life. Success was finally within my reach. All I had to do was call on the Law of Attraction, ask and willingly receive. Money fell like manna from heaven.

Trouble was, I wasn't paying a bit of attention to those pesky little guide signs along the way, the ones that screamed at me day and night. *Danger! Muy Peligroso! Ego Out of Control!* I was desperately ill and didn't know it. My work was becoming more difficult. More burdensome. More about making money. And less about helping others. It shames me to tell you all this, but that's where I was.

Of course, none of this mattered to me then. I knew I was set. Made in the shade. Fixed for life. My ego had taken complete control of my life. I didn't have time to consider health as a benefit. I was spending all my time buying Hawaiian shirts and giving orders. I wasn't painting. I wasn't writing. I couldn't. I still had a greater fortune to seek. It is only now as I write this book and my self-delusional fog begins to lift that I can see my plight and my immense need for healing. It's only now that I even see healing as the real benefit.

Ego Makes Fools Of Us All

Lying there in that Emergency Room all I allowed myself to think about was how lucky I was, how blessed I was. Hey, I was home free as long as I kept a positive mental attitude. Once again, I had faced disaster and walked away unscathed. Once again, I had defused a potentially bad situation solely with my inherent Irish luck and the power of my mind.

Oh, Dear God, no! It's happening again.

"Quick, Penelope, take my picture. It'll be funny. We'll use it in a promo."

"Dad, are you having another stroke? I don't want to take a picture now."

"Come on. We'll laugh about it later."

I could feel the seizure taking hold of my body. This time, however, there was nothing even remotely funny about it. I certainly wasn't laughing when my daughter snapped that picture. In fact, I can't even look at that picture today. Instantly, the right side of my body contracted involuntarily, radically, painfully. Very painfully. Like a giant body cramp from hell that never ends. Breathing was impossible. My mind filled with dread. All I could think of was saying goodbye to Diane. Would I get the chance?

Suddenly, the room was full of doctors and nurses. A giant electrical harness was glued tight to my chest. Wires, machines, tubes and hands everywhere. Now, a red-hot force it seemed was crushing my heart while my body curled in on itself. I couldn't breathe. My pain was excruciating. In the lack of a heartbeat the ambiance of the room changed from playful to deadly.

Then, just as suddenly, worry, concern and pain were no longer part of my reality. I watched from above with absolute detachment as the ER pros worked diligently and doggedly to restore the proper readings to all their monitors. They pushed, probed, medicated and generally abused my poor body, but I felt nothing more than a passing curiosity for a world I was leaving behind.

I never heard "Code Blue" echo through the corridors. I don't know how long they worked on me. Could have been an hour, could have been a few seconds. None of that mattered to me anyway because I had lost all interest in their efforts. I was concentrating on a far more compelling vision, a vision charged with light and wonder and incredible power just above me. A Power so pervasive I dared not question. A Power upon which I could not even look because to do so would ....

Hold On! Stop The Presses!

I confess I have a great deal of trouble writing about this part. It is still intensely painful for me to remember the details of what happened. I guess I haven't completely processed it yet. All will be revealed, I promise. But first let me fill in a little back-story. It would be unfair to tell you what happens next without first preparing you for the gift you asked me to bring back for you. Otherwise you'll never understand exactly how to heal yourself. How much healing you need before you can have your own Miracle. And why that's vitally important not just for you, but for your children, their children and their children's children. Why your need for healing extends as a thread through the tapestry of all there is and all there ever will be. I hope to present enough pertinent information that you recognize and desire your own desperate and immediate need for healing.

CHAPTER 3

Who Am I?

Writer? Salesman? Artist? Internet marketer? New Age Guru? I'm not sure my family would agree with that last one. I think they have a totally different opinion of who I am. At least, that's the impression I get by what they say and how they act. Whatever happened to a man being king in his own castle?

I don't think I agree with that guru thing either. To me, I'm just an ordinary guy. At heart, I'm still that skinny, truck driving kid back in Lincoln, Nebraska. Although, the truth is, like everybody, I'm many things. I've worn many hats and carried many handles. Probably the most difficult designation for me to accept most of my life, however, was explained to me by a very insightful friend and student.

"You are not a leader by choice. You are a leader by default. You see things which need doing and no one is doing them, so you take over."

That is the definition my friend and former student, Charles Burke, gave me at an Internet conference in Dallas when I was just getting started teaching on-line. I like this definition. I find it flattering. It also feels very close to the essence of who I am. The fact that he was reading my palm at the time adds a delightful spice to the story.

I do address issues that I think are in dire need of address-ing. I really can't help it. It's part of who I am. Diane and I had lunch with a rather strong-willed Irish nun during a healing conference in Vancouver a few years later. We talked about this concept, and she agreed that "leadership by default" was indeed my nature. She, however, attributed this quality to my heritage. She said, "Of course! You cannot abide injustice. You're Irish. You see injustice and you must do something about it. Simple as that."

Apparently, she believes being Irish is synonymous with lead-ership. But who's going to argue with a Mother Superior? Not me. And I'm not even Catholic.

Leader or not, I was ill equipped to deal with the economic crash of 2008. I had no answer to my students who asked why the Law of Attraction seemed like it wasn't working anymore. We could only watch helplessly as banks failed and housing prices came crashing down. Millions of people lost their jobs and their homes. Businesses dropped like flies. The U.S. govern-ment bailed out the banks and the businesses they deemed "too big to allow to fail." Hard times cascaded around the globe and down on those least able to withstand its effects. Ordinary folks like you and me had to bear the financial brunt of this debacle while a privileged few made billions of dollars and seemed to secure an even tighter control over our lives. I wanted an answer. I wanted to know what we could do about this outside con-trol over our lives. What could we do to counter the negative actions of others directly affecting our lives? All the cheating, the manipulating, the lying, the wheeling and dealing with our God-given birthright of a rich and happy life.

To me this is unconscionable. This is a cataclysm with a

magnitude on the human Richter scale of 10.0. The anger I feel because of all the needless human pain and suffering ignites my Irish wrath. This ongoing abuse of the many by the privileged few is unjust and needs attending.

The question is how do you attend to such a mammoth and all-encompassing chain of events such as the "Great Recession of 2008?" Which by official decree is long over and in recovery. (Boy, if you believe that, have I got a bridge for you.) That Great Recession was only the beginning of the most recent wave of encroachment on the welfare of the many by the few. The top one percent of humanity owns more assets than the bottom ninety-nine percent combined. They have the gold, which by old world standards means they make the rules for the rest of us. As far as I can tell, they don't seem to tip the scales much in our favor. So what can we do? Well, the simple answer is, it seems like there is nothing we can do. It seems like these things are simply above our pay grade.

Just because something seems true does not mean that it is true. It does not mean that at all.

Before the Great Recession people everywhere felt good about themselves and their future. Many more than today. They were brimming with hope. They felt as though they could affect change. They believed folks like me who proclaimed in conferences, preached from pulpits and declared on the Internet that You Can Get Anything You Want In Life by simply asking and receiving. A process that worked exceedingly well for anyone who sincerely tried it.

Lonely people found their Divine Complement. Workers found jobs. Wage earners became millionaires. The desperately ill found healing.

Why not now? These things are your birthright.

Now there are far too many good people struggling to make ends meet, feed their families and pay their bills. Honest, hard-working people for whom realization of the success they once felt deep inside is only a fading hope. You won't see them on TV. Those folks and those images don't sell toothpaste or beer. Although they are the reason why you see all the ads for new prescription drugs to calm your anxiety, put you to sleep and take away all your pain.

When you can no longer easily attract the Good Life you came here to live, then it is time to accept that something is desperately wrong. Accept that you must do something about it. Because like it or not, this world is not in the shape it is in as a result of dishonest government, greedy corporations or some mysterious evil lurking in the shadows.

No, we are in the shape we're in today because you and I are not doing our part.

We cannot blame Brazil, the World Bank or multinational corporations for the deforestation of the Amazon and creating catastrophic worldwide climate change as a result. They may be financing the destruction, but they are not to blame.

We cannot blame China, Wall Street, or even Swiss bankers for destroying the economy, lowering our standard of living and creating a scarcity consciousness among those who once believed in a world of unlimited abundance.

We cannot blame Islam, the Catholic Church, the World Health Organization or "dark forces" of the underworld for the acute and growing problems of overpopulation, grinding poverty and starvation among a full third of the world's population.

No! These are problems only we can solve. You and I.

Oh, don't get me wrong. These are not problems we can possibly solve in a conventional manner. If that were the case, they would have been solved long ago by people a lot smarter than I am. The only way these problems can and will be solved is by engaging a higher level of change.

Scarcity Consciousness

Both the few and the many suffer from the same basic problem: Scarcity Consciousness. From the time you began to understand how the world works you were taught that the one overriding factor controlling life is scarcity. You can't have a new bike, the toys you want, the food you want, the clothes you want or do the things you want to do because there's not enough money, there's not enough room in the closet, there's not enough time. You can only have so much because supply is limited. Now, this is true at a purely temporal level. There is only a limited supply of raw land, fresh water, food and hours in the day. The problem is we tend to extrapolate the mundane conditions of planet earth and apply them to how the world works. This kind of thinking is spiritually abhorrent to the good you desire to create. It is having a disastrous effect on your well-being and abundance.

Whether you believe you cannot have anything you want, or whether you believe you cannot have enough of what you want, either way, you suffer from a scarcity consciousness.

You start believing only in what you can see, touch, feel, taste and hear. This is the greatest disadvantage anyone can have.

Because you come to set limits for yourself. Limitations on the Infinite!

Your acknowledgement of lack leads to an understanding of all that you think you cannot have and eventually a belief in not having.

Ask and receive becomes want, but cannot have.

Healing And Infinite Abundance

Once you embody the Infinite Awareness of Creation within your being, you become immune to the ravages of lack. Lack ceases to exist. Ask and receive becomes instantaneous. Joy and well-being rule your earthly experience.

How you come to possess the Infinite Awareness of Creation, and what that ultimately means, is the golden ring waiting for those who are willing to extend themselves and expand their consciousness.

The only possible solution to the impossibly huge problems we face as a civilization is the exact same solution that heals and enriches both you and me. The simplicity of this solution is hard to believe and for me, at least, it was even harder to accept. I avoided talking about it for five years. Some guru. The guy who wrote The First Rule Of Prosperity: All Your Good Comes From God. Who for years said, "The real secret to a rich, happy and healthy life is surrendering your will to the will of God."

I malingered.

I found every excuse possible to avoid talking about what I learned in my death experience. I even claimed I couldn't remember, exactly.

As if anyone could forget a meeting with the Generous One.

I malingered because the solution was frighteningly simple. So simple I feared that you would dismiss it as a hoax and me as a charlatan and fraud. I crawled into a hole of self-delusion and focused on and blamed my physical handicaps. My white hair. My slow one-handed typing. My low energy. My weakened right arm and leg. Waaaah, I had a stroke! I blamed everything and everybody else in the world for my failure to keep the promise I made before I came back.

I malingered on my promise to God, because the job seemed too big for me. Above my station. Out of my reach. By deciding I wasn't good enough to do the job He, Himself, gave me, I denied both of us the Wisdom of Eternity. I put myself above the Source of All Wisdom and Knowledge. I showed pride before God to all eternity.

Not a good decision.

I cannot, however, avoid it any longer, not for another instant. Not in the middle of the day or the middle of the night. Because this is my mission. I came back with this simple message to deliver. A message of hope, love and healing. It's not difficult and it's not easy. It is very, very simple.

Elevate your own consciousness, now!

This is the road to every good thing you have ever desired for yourself, for your loved ones and for your kind. Humankind.

Because as you elevate your own consciousness, you raise the consciousness of the world. First, you affect those closest to you, then those who live near you, then those you know, then all those you don't know. In action this happens faster than the speed of light. In fact, it happens beyond the realm of speed and light. We'll talk more about that later.

Ultimate Win/Win

Here's the best part. All you have to do to elevate your consciousness is become the person you are here to be. Which is your right and your obligation to yourself. Become the person who lives the life you know in your heart you deserve to live. Become the person you've always wanted to be.

Elevate yourself and humankind will elevate with you. Inescapably. Decisively. Permanently. Little by little and bit by bit. By employing your elevated consciousness in everything you do, you engage the Universal tractor beam of good from which no group, corporation, institution nor individual is immune. Your world will become more abundant, more loving and infinitely more peaceful.

Elevating your consciousness will inevitably lead you to grasping the high station of your purpose. This will give you a level of satisfaction and of eternal gratitude which I cannot fully comprehend myself, let alone adequately describe or explain. Bliss is the only word I can find that approaches the feeling I had when it was shown to me.

The bottom line is, as you elevate your own life you elevate all of humanity. Conversely, as more and more folks elevate their lives they, too, pull you ever onward, ever forward, ever upward. You develop a completely symbiotic relationship with all humanity both individually and jointly. It is the ultimate win/win scenario. Rich folks and poor folks. Happy and sad folks. Good folks and bad folks. Christian. Moslem. Jew. Hindu. Buddhist. Baha'i. Atheist and agnostics, too. Everyone everywhere. No one can resist the power of you elevating your consciousness. Because elevating your consciousness draws you ever closer to the Ultimate Power of the Universe.

You are essential to this organic, this natural and Divine healing process. In fact, it's why you are here at this exact place and time. Now, let there be no mistake. This elevation process will happen with or without you. Of course, our degree of success and the speed of that success lie in the balance. But just like me, you get to decide for yourself whether you're in or out. That's the real beauty of this world. We all have free will.

All I can tell you is, I'm all in.

One Overriding Question

If elevating yourself is as simple as becoming the person you are here to be, how is that done? How do you go about becoming the person you are meant to become? If that's how you elevate yourself, how exactly do you do that?

Well, it starts with answering for yourself the seemingly simple, yet very complex question:

Who Am I?

CHAPTER 4
Chasing Rabbits

This is probably a good time to tell you the huge lingering effect of having a big dead spot in my brain. The stroke was on my left side, meaning that's where the dead spot is. The physical effects are mostly on the right, weakness and forty percent paralysis of my right arm, shoulder, leg, liver, mouth, throat, voice box, all the stuff on the right side of the body. Then there are the cognitive issues. The left side of the brain controls order, names, addresses, organizing skills, spelling and grammar. Things I've never been really good at anyway.

The good news is now they're all worse.

One of my first Quantum Selling students, an ex-minister, now selling insurance to businesses, called me "the biggest rabbit chaser in the world." If you've ever been pheasant hunting and the dog ignores pheasants while he chases rabbits, you'll know exactly what my friend means. He claimed I had a hard time staying on point. He was right of course, although I refer to it as random access. Even before my stroke, I wrote and taught from the right side of my brain, the creative side. And that, my friends, is how this book is written.

Stamp Out Hard Work!

It turns out, however, this is the way we learn the fastest with the most retention. It's a more natural flow of information. Logic-based learning makes learning hard work. Something I am absolutely opposed to doing. Random access learning is how children learn before we impose our outdated, left-brain, top-down educational paradigm on them. They learn best by playing. Kids run from one thing that interests them to another, taking what they want and need. Random access learning is intuitive rather than cognitive. That's how I write. I go from one thing to another, trying to keep things light and fun. Mix it up a little. Keep everything interesting and still reveal vital information. My hope is that way you will be drawn to what you need or desire. That way you will be engaged and having fun so you are open to new information.

In 1999, Sugata Mitra, a Ph.D. in physics and the head of research at a $2 billion software and education company in India, launched a study he calls "minimally invasive education." He started by embedding a computer connected to high speed Internet in a wall in a slum in New Delhi. He turned the computer on and left it there. His results were breathtaking.

Since then, he has extended the experiment to poor places all over the world. Over the years Sugata found that illiterate children (age range 6 to 12), if left alone, would learn anything they find interesting, very quickly. They had no teachers. No planned lessons. No tests to quantify their progress. They had only computers, the Internet and their own desire to follow what interests them.

They learned to surf the web almost immediately. Within hours one group wrote and recorded their own music and played it back. Within weeks another group who had never even heard English spoken, learned how to speak it without an accent. Another group learned the basics of DNA research. These were all dirt poor, uneducated children ages six to twelve! Dr. Mitra has a video on Ted Talks. I recommend you watch it. It may cause you to question more than your ideas on education.

What would the world be like in ten or twenty years if every child on Earth had access to a computer and the Internet? Could we end some of these dreadfully menacing problems we have now? Could one of these forgotten kids in the third world cure cancer, AIDS, dementia or even old age? Create sustainable fission? Bend time and space, opening the doorway to the exploration of distant galaxies?

Let's do it! Right? What are we waiting for? Write your congressman, donate a couple bucks, get business on board. Let's start putting this amazing new idea to work immediately! Couldn't cost more than a few hundred billion. The U.S. military goes through that faster than you know what goes through a goose.

Good idea, but we all know that it's not going to happen on a large enough scale to be effective. Because of one Universal law: For every action there is an equal but opposite reaction. The effects of implementing Sugata Mitra's plan of children educating themselves is not workable given the state of health in the world today.

Universities and teachers' unions would go ballistic the minute these "new schools" affected their student memberships and their own livelihood. Kids learning that quickly without their help could put them out of business overnight. Congress isn't about to spend taxpayer money educating children in another country. It's not their purview. War, of course, is good business.

They can sell that back home, get support, press, and contributions, which gets them re-elected in a landslide. But educating the Third World? Forget it! They'd never see another term. Voters wouldn't stand for it. They don't want to spend money on their own kids. Let Africans pay for their children! Oh, and what happens when people at the height of their careers with kids in college, a mortgage and two car payments start losing their jobs to sixteen-year-olds? How would you feel if that happened to you?

As much as I hate to say this: Revolutionary ideas like radical education reform are doomed to the dustbin of great ideas that didn't make it until we deal with a much deeper issue. The cornucopia of good that seems to await us at every turn will have to wait. There's only one problem, but it's a big one.

We are simply not ready or willing to receive this level of abundance.

Divine Alignment Enables Healing

I fervently believe that I can have anything I want in life, if I simply ask and willingly receive. It's our birthright! Ordained by God! And designed into our temporal matrix. But the thing is, it only occurs when we are in complete alignment with our desire. If you align completely with the energy of what you desire, it materializes in your life quickly, organically. You ask, you visualize what you desire, you detach and let the Universe do the heavy lifting. Bingo! Your desire shows up in your life. This is a very short hand version of the system we teach on RichDreams. com. You do this to a greater or lesser degree every day. Usually without thinking much about it. This works best when you are focusing your desire on simple things like a new car or a new home, because you can easily align with these things. As long as you keep your requests simple and detailed without getting overly demanding (like asking for your neighbors' house) these requests are easily attainable. More complicated desires, like moving to a higher level of abundance involving other humans, a loving, healthy and prosperous family, or a kind and peaceful world environment are more challenging. This requires not only your alignment with a more elevated or transcendent truth, but the alignment of a larger and more elevated group consciousness.

See, we cannot ask for others. You wouldn't want somebody else deciding the life they think you should live, right? So, none of us are allowed to ask for others. That means real changes in our culture must come from a significant group asking for compatible desires. That is not, however, the impossible task you may imagine. Actually, it is much easier than it seems.

Most of us think of healing as it applies to fixing our bodies. Returning our physical form to its original, whole state after damage has been inflicted upon it. Fixing us or someone else. We think in terms of blood and bones, of surgery and treatment, of prevention and cure, of pills and diet. These temporal fixes have no effect on the real challenges and purposes you came into this life to face and resolve. The Miracle Healing, the deep and abiding healing we propose here is exactly what is needed to bring you and eventually all of humankind into alignment with higher truth. Which will manifest in a glorious and higher level of abundance, a loving healthy family, and a kind and peaceful world environment in which we can all prosper and thrive.

We have to heal individually to fix the economy, to encourage creative expression, to allow freedom of education and information. To honor the sanctity of the individual, and his or her right to become the most he or she can become. To become the assct that God ordained us to be regardless of where we live, whom we know, or how that impacts the bottom line. To make decisions balancing our own good and the good of humanity in mind. To treat friends like family, and family like friends. Of course, this is not completely possible today. Our civilization is desperately ill and we must heal it before we can have that happy ending we all want.

Now, here's the good part. All this fixing the world stuff is simple once you understand the nature of this elevated healing.

As I have said, the Miracle Healing I brought back is much bigger and more pervasive than getting over a cold or learning to walk after a stroke. Healing realigns the body from the inside out. Our civilization is no different; it also heals from the inside out. And you are the catalyst that can make that happen.

Healing on every level is the re-establishing of the natural order of things. It is a process that allows Divine truth to bloom within our lives and our world. By healing the individuals, you eventually heal the world, as we talked about last chapter. Healing works by bringing the whole body into balance. Not by pushing against resistance, but by inspiring the harmony intrinsic to the system. All systems have a natural order. So healing the world is not about changing the world, but allowing the natural order to emerge.

All we have to do to heal the world is heal ourselves. Easy-Peezy Lemon-Squeezy. Actually, it does take some effort and desire, but the rewards are endless. Think of the leprechaun legend and that magical pot of gold at the end of every rainbow. How finding it opens every door and satisfies your every desire.

Healing yourself is better than that and so much easier to do and enjoy.

Of course, we can continue to ignore the call for healing that is currently screaming at us from every corner of humanity. Just watch the evening news. Ignore the pain, discomfort and constant deterioration of our physical, mental and spiritual well-being. And continue down the same path we've been on for thousands of years. A path dominated by prejudice, hate, violence, conflict, control and manipulation. A path that has grown from a trail into what is now a super-high-speed toll way with fewer and fewer opportunities to exit while every day the toll climbs higher and higher.

You simply tell yourself none of that disgusting chaos concerns you. You are immune. You are protected by your rank, race, nationality, financial condition or religion. You are an island, above and apart from the sea of troubles surrounding you. This is the myth of Separateness. Albert Einstein called it a kind of Optical Illusion of Consciousness.

> "A human being is a part of the whole, called by us 'the Universe,' a part limited in time and space. He experiences himself, his thoughts and feelings, as something separate from the rest – a kind of optical delusion of consciousness. This delusion is a kind of prison for us, restricting us to our personal desires and affection for a few persons nearest to us. Our task must be to free ourselves from this prison by widening the circle of understanding and compassion to embrace all living creatures and the whole of nature in its beauty."

To think for one minute that people you love and people you fear or despise and people you don't even know are somehow separate from you is human folly. There is nothing separate about us. We are one. You, me, terrorists, the ultra-rich, those in grinding poverty, fire ants, brilliant new ideas, the Pacific Ocean, far distant galaxies. We are all one. Everything you do, think and feel has an effect on everyone and everything else. Just as everything they do has an effect on you. You may not always notice the effect, but it's there all the same. Sometimes the effect on the whole is seemingly miniscule, like when you think about buying a new pair of shoes or how you feel about Oktoberfest. Sometimes it's huge and far reaching like Orville Wright's 12 second, heavier-than-air manned flight at Kitty Hawk, North Carolina, at 10:35 a.m. on December 17, 1903. So import-ant we actually remember the exact time, date and place. And sometimes it is an effort with so many contributors and such a long growth path that we don't even ask the question. "Who invented the internet?"

Of course, you never know what effect your actions will have or how far reaching they will be. When the effect of my sixth stroke was burning through my body I certainly wasn't thinking, "Oh goodie, I'm dying. Now, I'll have new material for another book. Maybe I can help someone else." No, I was thinking ... well, I better not say.

There is no separation. There is no you and I. There is no physical, mental or emotional separation in time and space between any of us. What happens in India has an immediate effect in New Jersey, although maybe unseen and unnoticed. This Universal Law, this quantum level cause and effect, is a proven fact of science as absolute and dependable as the sun-rise. Walk into a wedding party and feel how you are instantly affected. Or a funeral. Or remember how you felt on September

11, 2001. We are one. We cannot be separated. You cannot be separated from anyone, anywhere, anytime. You and I are held fast by invisible yet unyielding bonds not just to each other, but to those Paleolithic cave painters in Lascaux, France, and those elevated folks who will one day teleport between planets and starships. We are all one. Still we persist in believing we are somehow separate.

Please note that from what I've witnessed, the path of separateness does not have a happy destination. Fortunately, you can choose a better path, and it all starts with getting a healthy body, mind and spirit. Healing your body, mind and spirit is no small feat. It takes effort. There are no magic pills you can take and be instantly cured. And it doesn't happen overnight. I am a perfect example of that. It took me over five years to start writing this book after a lifetime of overcoming obstacles and doing what needed doing. I am a writer. This is my stock and trade. Along with my daughter, Penelope Pauley, I've created books and courses, which push out the boundaries of possibility and encourage you to believe in yourself and become all that you can be. This book should have been a snap. It's what, 60,000 – 70,000 words? That should take me about eight to twelve weeks for a rough draft. That's 1,200 words or five doubled spaced pages a day six days a week for twelve weeks granting corrections – three months tops. A piece of cake! So why did I wait five long years? And why did it take so darn long to complete?

Because I simply wasn't ready.

I had a lot to learn. That's the bottom line on why we are living at this time and in this place. We all have a lot to learn, regardless of what we know or think we know. Think of this as growing into the person you were always meant to be. The hero's quest. So, when the frustration gets thick and success looks doubtful there's only one option. Rejoice! You are living in the most glorious space-time planet Earth has ever hosted. You have chosen to live now! You have the skills and power to help forge the greatest civilization ever known to humankind, the gateway to a glorious and bountiful future. Not just in material ways, but just as importantly, in spiritual ways. Because without spiritual advancement, the material gains are destined to fade into a sunset that has no sunrise.

You have to work through all the difficulties in front of you. That's just the way it is. Pushing doesn't work. Anger certainly doesn't work. Bad language, long hours, careless driving or self-abasement, nothing can speed your progress. Only allowing works.

I know because I tried them all.

Only now have I grown enough to write this book. And each new chapter seems to initiate new and increasingly more difficult challenges, tests and difficulties. Imagine if God told you to do something. Maybe he told you it was your mission, and all you had to do to accomplish this mission was to trust Him above all things. Trust Him above your own senses. Trust Him above what you knew to be true. Trust Him above the laws of physics and the common sense you have learned through the School of Hard Knocks. Then imagine He said: "Walk across the water to that boat." What would you do? Would you try? Would you turn around and give up? Or would you walk across the water like His Holiness Christ did?

Boy, that would take some heavy-duty trust. I'm not ready to walk on water either, although at times, what's asked of me seems about that challenging. I'm sure you know what I mean.

We, each and every one, are given challenges consistent with our own station and ability to achieve.

I don't know all the answers. All I can do is share what I've been given with you. Maybe you'll glean something that will help you.

Wait! There is one more thing I must admit before we go farther. One thing that kept me from writing more than any other, at least, overtly. Maybe it was the excuse for all the real problems. "How can I tell you I died when clearly I didn't?" Because dead men don't write books. Well, most don't anyway.

Seriously, I've spent four years worrying about that instead of celebrating my miracle life. What a dummy! OK, I walk funny. I don't have the energy to do everything anymore. I can't type with my right hand, yet. The mere thought of joining friends on a river rafting expedition scares the Dickens out of me. But I'm here. I do walk. I do type. I do have fun. I do have a good 4-6 hours of work a day in me. I'm not lying in a bed somewhere drooling my life away. And even if I were, I am sure there's something I could do or know or accomplish. Life is too precious to waste a minute.

Thank you, God!!!

I am going to tell the whole impossible mystery of my death and miracle life even if it means we transverse the quantum realm for clarification. Which isn't nearly as complicated and mysterious as it seems once you take away all the big words scientists love. My story may at the very least give you hope. Hope that you can best any difficulty, overcome any apparent obstacle and live your life with the strength, determination and confidence that comes from knowing that a Higher Power lies within you. Waiting for your acceptance.

Or maybe it will encourage you to accept who you are, where you are, and embrace the Good the Universe has bestowed upon you. Regardless of what it feels like, looks like or seems like. Recognize that life is one big bag of illusions – all for your benefit.

Now, as Sir Arthur Conon Doyle so aptly put it, "The game is afoot." Let us go, then, you and I, on a quest for the essence of healing. Find the greatest talisman to change, power and true abundance. Because all the money, power and stuff in the world means less than a big bag full of sugar pills if you are sick, diseased or worse yet, dead.

CHAPTER 5

Worst Of Days

I had just celebrated my birthday, which was the best of days. Actually, it was my birthday and St. Patrick's Day combined. We do that because my granddaughter, Lucy, is also a Pisces and her birthday is very close to mine. How can you go wrong when your celebration is joined with the worldwide jubilation generated by St. Patrick's Day? Impossible, right? Erin Gaugh Braugh!

Leave it to me. I found a way.

March 28, 2009, was the worst of days. Less than a fortnight after my birthday, I got up early and took my wife to catch a 6:45 a.m. flight to El Paso, Texas. She was going to see her 92-year-old mother, Dorothy. Her mother was living in Hobbs, New Mexico, at the time. Diane flew to El Paso, Texas. From there she had a five to six hour drive across desert and mountain terrain all by herself.

I didn't want her to go. I had this strange feeling all week. I couldn't shake it. Diane really wanted to see her mother and she loved that long, lonely drive. I was afraid something would happen to her. She said it was her only private time. She said it was refreshing and rejuvenating. How could I argue with that? Besides once Diane decides to do something, she's not easily swayed.

She never got farther than El Paso.

After dropping Diane off at John Wayne Airport I went back home to finish writing a book I'd started three years earlier. Like most of my work the idea for this book came in a flash of inspiration and a frantic hour or two of typing. Then something unusual happened. I got nothing for three years. Very frustrating. I hoped the ten days she was gone would give me enough alone time to reconnect with the energy of that book. I had a remarkable first chapter, an amazing story that I had completely forgotten, a story that explained the role a mass murderer and a pickpocket played in my becoming a Quantum Master and teacher.

At this writing, I still haven't finished that book.

It was dark when I arrived back home. My dog, Tobee, had passed a year earlier and the house was deathly quiet without Diane. I turned on Sports Center and fried a couple of eggs. I let my ancient cat, Onyx, out the patio door. I took a minute to glance out on the pool and my beloved yard, which fanned out like an amphitheater surrounded by a tropical verge. I remembered the parties, the rock and roll bands, the great barbeques and all the good friends. If anything should inspire me, it was that back yard. But it didn't inspire, encourage or give me any degree of solace or comfort.

I was totally caught up with what I didn't have. I was dwelling on the one thing I often admonished my students to ban from their thinking. I was focused on the worst possible energy on the planet. I was focused on the one thing that destroys hope and possibility and keeps you from having all the good in your life.

I was focused on lack.

I didn't have a new book. I'd never been on Oprah. I didn't enjoy selling from the stage. I wasn't growing the list fast enough. I wasn't developing new products. I wasn't promoting. I wasn't expanding. I wasn't growing. I wasn't selling enough. I wasn't making enough money. All the while, we were struggling to get by on a monthly income a great many people would love to make in a year.

Naturally, I didn't see my own ingratitude. I couldn't. Because all I saw was lack. I had allowed a scarcity consciousness to take root in my incredibly successful life. I wasn't good enough. I wasn't smart enough. I wasn't connected enough. I saw myself as a failure, a ne'er-do-well, a pretender. Oh, then there were the bank failures. Hurricane Katrina. The housing crash. World hunger. Lost jobs. The Great Recession.

I felt responsible for all of it because I was playing God.

I should have been singing, *I'm Rich Beyond My Wildest Dreams. I am. I am. I am.* Our life was an absolute joy! But instead, I was focused on materialism and greed. Me! The Tom Pauley that proclaimed to the world the importance of giving thanks, never asking for money and living on the quantum or spiritual side of life.

I wasn't taking my own advice. Heavens, I couldn't even hear the truth any more. I had let my ego get completely out of control. I was pushing rather than allowing. This was the attitude with which I entered my office to finish that book.

Obviously, I was headed for a fall.

About 9:30 a.m., while sitting at my desk, I noticed my computer mouse was sticking. It came and went. But something was definitely wrong with my mouse. It just wouldn't move. As much as I tried to move that mouse, it stayed put. Now, I'm technically challenged so this didn't cause me much worry. I figured it was time for a green drink. Maybe the computer or the mouse or whatever was wrong would heal itself.

Besides, I was feeling nauseated and I took that to mean I was hungry. So, I grabbed an armful of fruits and veggies from the back refrigerator and headed for the kitchen to make a green drink. But when I stepped over the threshold from the garage, my right foot slapped to the floor and refused to move. For a few seconds I couldn't move my right leg.

I was dumbfounded. Why wouldn't my leg move? I had no idea why my leg wouldn't move. Or maybe, I refused to admit why my leg wouldn't move. The only possible answer was too absurd to consider.

Within a few seconds it did move and I went the ten steps to the kitchen. As I passed the patio door I saw that Onyx wanted in. I unlocked and opened the sliding door, but didn't get a chance to shut it because my entire right side stopped working.

I slumped into a chair, stunned. I was by now forced to admit to myself that something was dreadfully wrong with my body.

I sat for a minute or two looking at my right arm hanging there, refusing to move. I couldn't stand. I couldn't move anything on my right side. I reached around with my left hand and took my cell phone out of its holster and called my daughter, Penelope.

It was Saturday and I was surprised she actually took my call. She's protective of her time off. Claims I use the phone like a machine gun. Anyway she took the call. Our conversation went something like this.

"Yes, Dad, we're sitting down to breakfast. Can I call you back?"

"No, Pen, I think I'm having a stroke."

"That's nothing to joke about. I'll call you back in about 30 minutes."

"Pen, it's no joke. I think I'm having a stoke. I can't move my right side."

"Oh my God, call 911."

"Ah … well, I was wondering if you could come over."

"Dad, call 911. The paramedics will take you to a hospital."

"What are you talking about! I'm not paying for an ambulance. I'd have to be crazy to pay the kind of prices they charge. I want you to come and take me."

"Dad, I'm forty minutes away. If you won't call 911, get your neighbor Jacci to take you."

"I'm not going to bother her. Maybe I can drive."

"No! Dad, do not drive yourself. A stroke is very dangerous you could…."

"Oh, that's my other line. It's your mother; I hope she's OK. I'll call you back."

"Dad, call 911…." (Disconnect)

"Hi, Diane are you OK?"

"I'm fine. The plane just landed and I am about to get the rental car."

"Get a big one, that's a long drive."

"I already ordered a midsize. It'll be fine. How are you doing with the book?"

"Well, I had to stop because of the stroke."

"A stroke is nothing to joke about."

"That's what Penelope said. I can't move my right arm, and I don't think my leg will move either."

"Tom, call 911, right now."

It's too expensive. I'll drive to the hospital as soon as I can move my leg."

"Tom do you want me to come back?"

"Heavens no. Go see your mother. Enjoy yourself, I'll be fine."

"Tom, I'm calling Jacci. Hang up and call 911."

"Nonsense, you have a nice trip. Give everybody my love." (Disconnect)

I am sharing this absurd conversation with you because I want you to understand this very important fact: A stroke can make you instantly crazy or at the very least extremely irrational.

When I heard Jacci from next door pounding on the front door, I finally called 911. The operator told me two people had already called and the ambulance was on the way. She also told me to lie down on the floor on the side that was having the stroke, which was a bit confusing since I was having trouble telling one side from the other. But I did try to lie down. Unfortunately, it was more like falling than lying. I don't know if that was the best advice.

I can remember lying on the floor thinking how lucky I was to have left the patio door open, since all the other doors were locked. I didn't want them damaging that front door to get in. I'd painted it six times to get the color right.

Oh my, what I didn't know about strokes would fill a book. But then I'm not alone. Who the heck wants to study up on strokes if you're never going to have one, right?

Doctors don't seem to know much about strokes either. They know more than I do of course, but every time I asked them a question like how long, how fast, will it ever? They always had the same answer, "All strokes are different."

After what seemed like hours of yelling trying to get the Firemen who were ready to break down my door to come to the patio door, finally, one did. He wasn't real interested in how many times I painted the front door either. He did open it for the Emergency Medical Technicians. There were two of them, a good-looking guy and a beautiful young woman. She was strong as a horse. It really surprised me that a woman could lift me on to the gurney. She, in fact, did most of the heavy lifting. I guess our prejudices about women's equality run pretty deep.

They kept asking me the dumbest questions about the names of my medications. Who can pronounce all those strange names under the best conditions? They also asked about my experience with drugs. Neither one thought the Bill Clinton remark about not inhaling was the least bit funny. Man, what a tough audience. After they lifted me onto the gurney and strapped me in, I tried a Henny Youngman line. The woman asked me if I was comfortable. I said, *I make a good living*. Nothing. No laughs. No smiles. Nothing. It was like I was talking to myself. Hey, I was scared. My body wouldn't work right. This had to be some grotesque joke perpetrated by God the Humorous. I was just trying to keep things light.

It was not even close to light.

The EMTs had definitely had stroke patients before because they were all business. And very good at it, I must say. Jacci brought all my prescriptions down from our bathroom. I confirmed these were all my meds. And they wheeled me out to the ambulance while Jackie closed up the house.

Once I was settled in the ambulance, the heavens opened and the angels must have started singing because I could move my arm and leg again. I was ecstatic.

"Wait! Hold on, guys. It's all over. I can move again. Let me out. There's no need for me to go to the hospital. I'm fine."

"We're not allowed to do that, sir. Best let the doctors check you out. You could have just had a TIA. If so, they'll send you right home. Or it could be the precursor to a bigger event."

"But I am home. And I'm not going to have another event, I promise. All you have to do is untie me and I'll walk back to the house. Seriously. I'm fine."

If you are anywhere near somebody having a stroke, one word of advice, don't believe a word they say. I wasn't fine. In fact, I was the last person on earth to make that decision. I was a mess. Of course, I am a closer so I spent much of the trip to the hospital trying to talk them out of it. They stopped listening. I was left to watch the gleaming red fire truck behind me as our little convoy made its way through Saturday morning traffic down El Toro Road.

If I had been in a clear mind then I would have realized how much I had to be grateful for. My daughter in Orange, California, and my wife in El Paso, Texas, each made one phone call. Either of which would have brought two highly trained and competent EMTs, an ambulance, two firemen and a really cool fire truck to my door within 5 minutes. Diane, Penelope, Jacci, the EMTs and the Firemen, they saved my life. If I'd have been left to my own devices, I'd probably have died on my kitchen floor a few hours later. Or been trapped there in that condition until Monday morning, when folks started showing up for work.

I was given a gift I can never adequately explain. Still, I wasn't grateful. I was looking for the angle. Why was this happening to me of all people? Wasn't I one of the good guys? I was telling folks to let the Universe "open the doors, provide the means, make safe your path and guide your way." Do so and you can live a dream life. This wasn't a dream; it was a nightmare.

I was still focused on lack. Some people do not learn quickly. I was still under the delusion that my actions alone determined my success and failure. I believed that I was somehow separate from everything else in the Universe. I completely forgot that my greatest power is to surrender my will to the will of God. Oh I wrote and taught otherwise. But somewhere in the back of my mind I held on tight to my old antiquated belief in hard work and long hours. That whatever success I had was due to my own talent, luck and hard work.

I was in the position I was in because I had forgotten all the lessons that God had given me as confirmation of His infinite power. Especially, the lesson I learned so many years ago on a deserted mountain highway on a warm summer night. This was the lesson that should have wiped all doubt of God's power from my mind once and for all.

I had forgotten the true meaning of Infinite Possibility.

What Is Possible?

"Why, sometimes I've believed as many as six impossible things before breakfast."
The White Queen, Lewis Carroll's *Through The Looking Glass*

This often quoted passage has been used both to ridicule those who believed in new ideas and to praise those who kept an open mind.

The question is, where do you stand? Open or closed?

Are you like Alice when the Queen told her to consider that she was more than 101 years old? "There's no use trying," [Alice] said: "One *can't* believe impossible things."

Or are you like the White Queen? "I daresay you haven't had much practice," said the Queen. "When I was your age, I always did it for half-an-hour a day. Why, sometimes I've believed as many as six impossible things before breakfast."

I always thought I was like the Queen. Open minded. A free thinker. Not burdened by conventional wisdom. Maybe I just never grew up because I always believed anything was possible. That is until one dark night, alone with my thoughts, in the mountains. I saw something that changed forever how I understood what is possible and what is not.

CHAPTER 6
Starlight Weekend

It was almost 9:00 p.m. The sun had long ago since dropped below the southern crest of the rugged Sacramento Mountains of south central New Mexico. Moonrise wouldn't come until 5:00 a.m. and there wasn't a cloud in sight. The deep, deep darkness that comes to the mountains was fast approaching. I couldn't have had a more beautiful night for a long, reflective drive home at peace with the world and myself. Grateful to my core for all that we had gained by leaving the teeming hustle of the big city for the quickening power of wide-open spaces and earnest friendships. I certainly wasn't expecting to have my understanding of the nature of reality shattered in a matter of seconds. I've always believed without reservation that anything – absolutely anything is possible because we lived in a world of infinite abundance. I'd heard that all my life from people like me saying you could have anything you wanted. If it follows that you can have anything you want, then anything was possible. At least, I thought that's what I believed, until my belief was tested.

I was the only one awake as I sped along the winding mountain road in our full sized Plymouth sport van. It was my pride and joy, big, roomy and powered by one of those huge V8s that positively flew between gas stations. I loved that van and I loved driving it. The two thick bench seats in back folded down into beds, so Penelope, Alex and Heather could sleep, which happened almost as soon as we left Alamogordo. That was almost an hour ago, and we still had a good three and a half hours until we got home. Diane was asleep in the front passenger seat. She was going to keep me company, but she lasted only a little longer than the kids. Everybody was exhausted from the weekend. I was wide-awake. I was used to driving long distances. We did it at least once a month. Besides I had plenty to think about. In fact, I had never been so intellectually stimulated in my life.

In our mid-thirties, after filing our first bankruptcy, Diane and I sold nearly everything we owned, rented a truck and became modern day pioneers, forsaking Houston, Texas, for the little oil town of Hobbs, New Mexico. What a wonderful experience. I wouldn't trade it for the world. I ran the sales department for the area's two largest radio stations. With no TV stations for hundreds of miles, we were local media kings. Our family members were local celebrities. The kids did radio commercials. Diane starred in the Community Playhouse. One of us was in the paper or on the radio nearly every week. On weekends we traveled throughout West Texas, Southern New Mexico and Northern Mexico making friends and sharing a closeness that's impossible to explain. People seem to forge stronger bonds in the country than they do in the city.

We were heading home from a long weekend camping with about a hundred of our closest friends. I was tired, but still riding the spiritual high that comes from such a profound and elevating event. We spent three amazing days and two nights, renewing friendships and exploring the ancient mysteries of the Most Great Beauty while roughing it in the mountain wilds. It was very primitive. Very basic. OK, we had a large meeting hall, running water and hot showers, but we did sleep in tents and cook outdoors. That's pretty basic, right?

The night before, my good friend, Richard Gurinsky and I lay under the light of approximately seven point five billion trillion stars discussing physics and the nature of reality. The most generally accepted number of stars in the known universe is thirty billion trillion. Divide by four and you get the number of stars in the northern hemisphere at any one time, give or take a few trillion. Of course, you can't really see all those stars with the naked eye, but who's counting? Richard, whose dad had been on the Manhattan Project and helped develop the first atomic bomb, taught physics at a local university and had dedicated his life to improving the lot of the poor and underprivileged, primarily families along the Mexican-American border as well as Native American families on the Mescalero Apache reservation. I always felt that his work was a reaction to his father's legacy. It benefited not only the people he and wife, Margaret, touched, but humankind as a whole.

That definitely includes me, because it brought us all together. Richard and I had many world-class discussions. That night he introduced me to String Theory, which proposed the possibility of, at least, a ten dimensional universe. We spent a lot of time on the concept of a multiverse and how that manifests in our daily lives. We talk about this extensively in *Quantum Selling, A Revolutionary Course Of Action*.

At the time, I found the material stimulating, yet difficult to get my head around. This kind of discussion was not entirely new to me. I was always interested in knowing more about the Universe in which I lived. *Scientific American* was the only magazine I ever read consistently. I usually understood about one article out of ten. Richard, however, was an excellent teacher. With his help and the living example of the seven point five billion trillion stars above, I was served that night a taste of infinity. Richard used simple language and demonstrated with easy uncomplicated examples, making it possible for even a hardheaded Irish salesman like myself to understand the most complicated subjects. Oh, he wasn't perfect by any means. He could be a royal pain in the get-along. He was a classic narcissist. He thought he knew all there was to know. He thought he was always right. He always wanted to control everything. He was much like me. Probably why we got along so well. God bless his soul. Richard passed very young. Sometimes, I think he's still with me, helping me understand challenging problems.

Looking at that impossibly large number of stars, without mentioning galaxies, star clusters, nebula, molecular gas clouds, black holes, quasars, supernovas, red giants, white dwarfs, star nurseries, asteroids, comets, planets, moons – oh, and let us not forget dark matter, because dark matter constitutes 95 percent of the total content of the universe, I was definitely challenged mentally. To look at that God-given vision and realize that it is only an infinitesimally tiny piece of a speck of our infinite universe makes you rethink everything you thought you once knew. At least, it did me. It is impossible for the finite mind to even imagine the infinite. By keeping an open mind it is possible to accept as true what you cannot see, touch, feel, hear, or smell. I made a quantum leap in my thinking that night.

No, it was more than that. I realized for the first time what believing in infinite possibility really meant. It meant accepting the things, the concepts and ideas I could never totally understand as possible. Even if I wasn't comfortable with what that meant.

If you've not lain under a cloudless, moonless summer sky in a place far away from the diminishing effect of city lights, do yourself a favor and do this, at least once in your life. Let the light of that living example burn an image of infinity permanently into your mind. It is amazing how your consciousness grows exponentially under the guidance of billions of trillions of stars. Maybe Richard will even whisper some new ideas in your mind as you watch.

Until then, imagine you are there right now. Open your mind and picture what I am describing. Picture the unadulterated night sky on a cloudless, moonless night far away from city lights. Then imagine yourself traveling beyond this universe, to another one just as deep and just as impossibly large and then another and then another and another until the number of universes you visit is beyond your scope of comprehension.

This is an introduction to infinity.

Exercise One:
Envisioning Infinity

The exercise you are about to do is exceeding simple. My grandson did this for me when he was four without the slightest hesitation. He thought it was fun. My granddaughter was eight when she did it. She thought it was "kinda lame" because we didn't do more, but then she's been meditating since she was four. You can do this exercise. I know you can. My only concern is that you might also think it's kinda lame and don't give it the respect it deserves.

This exercise is incredibly important. It is like learning to control your breathing when you start meditating. Most people want to skip right over that and go on to the good stuff. Of course, the good stuff cannot possibly happen until you learn how to control your breathing.

It is vitally important that you need a vision, a visceral understanding of the endless reaches of this universe if you are ever going to envision the infinite. Which is essential for you to accept the powerful gift I have brought back for you. The gift of Miracle Healing.

Technically, it is impossible for the finite mind to comprehend the infinite, so we must resort to a little trickery. Since your mind does not know it cannot imagine infinity (minds do anything we ask them to), we are going to give your mind an image to use as a launch site for our quantum travels in the coming chapters.

In all seriousness pretend you are four again and do this simple exercise without thinking. Just relax and open your mind to infinite possibility.

Find a quiet place where you won't be disturbed for a couple of short minutes. Relax your mind and body. Let the stresses and responsibilities of your day vanish like the morning fog. Turn off all electronic devices. Close your eyes and take three deep breaths. Now imagine yourself on that mountaintop in New Mexico or by a lake in the north woods with an unobstructed view of creation. If you are a science fiction fan, see yourself aboard the Starship Enterprise traveling at something less than warp speed.

See for yourself the beautiful and rich expanse of our universe and beyond. Watch the galaxies, nebula and all the many wonders of space stream past on your mental journey to the end of the visible universe and beyond. Remember: Your mind may not be able to comprehend infinity, but it doesn't know that. It will do what you ask. So ask to see the infinite and immense, sensual reality of creation right now.

Do this now. It will be good practice when I ask you to imagine The Arc of Light when we prepare for your gift. But don't think about that now. Close your eyes and imagine the infinite expanse of our universe. The rest of the book will mean more to you once you complete this simple exercise.

CHAPTER 7
On The Road Again

Now, if you recall, I was driving home from a relaxing, mind-expanding weekend in the mountains. The sun had set and it was deep, deep, blindingly forest dark. Diane and the kids were asleep in the big van as I thundered along the solitary, two-lane mountain road. I was tired, but charged with the energy of the great weekend and pondering my new understanding of what infinite possibility really meant.

Of course, my lesson was strictly theoretical. To me it still meant I had a lot of options should I choose to take them. My understanding revolved completely around me. I felt infinitely (am I over using this word?) smarter than I had before the camping trip, which was as it should be because the entire camping experience was all about me (the ego never quits). What I didn't know was that another lesson was coming my way. In some ways it was simpler, almost comical. Now, this would be a great relief from all this talk of stars, galaxies and trillions of alternative universes if it had not been for an ultimately far more challenging and downright frightening lesson just ahead.

All I knew was the weekend was over and I was going home. Lessons were over, time for work. Sure, my body was tired and you can make a case that what I saw was an exhaustion-induced hallucination, but I'm not buying that. I was awake and alert. My mind was clear. What I saw was what I saw. I believe what I saw was one of many life elevating experiences we all receive all the time if we open our hearts and minds to accept them. Unfortunately, we often dismiss the more challenging experiences out of fear of what we don't understand.

I was rounding one of the many blind curves, the mountain dropping off on my right and the Mexican AM radio station playing brightly when my lesson came. The proof, perhaps, for the lesson Richard began the night before. Now I only saw this magical vision for a couple of seconds, but it was powerful. This unexpected and impossible example of infinite possibility landed directly in the path of the strong running lights I had installed just before this trip.

I had an exceedingly good look.

I was caught completely off guard. There was no warning. But that's always how it is when God sends us a lesson. We don't have time to prepare our defenses. If I knew this lesson was coming I'd have quickly donned the armor of common wisdom, so I could deflect, deny or refute what I saw. I've always claimed to be open to new ideas, new possibilities, but in truth, nobody wants to have their core beliefs challenged. Which is exactly what this particular lesson did for me. Naturally, I had to be caught off guard. That way the lesson could and would sink in.

It appeared in a flash, an animal as tall as my van, weighing well over four hundred pounds, the color of a mule deer. He jumped onto the highway. Only it clearly wasn't a mule deer. I've seen plenty of them. This animal was one of a kind, one that could not possibly exist. Except it did exist. I saw it. It was an impossible idea in the flesh.

I immediately realized the danger. My adrenalin was pumping faster than my Plymouth V8 could suck that high-octane fuel. I was terrified. I'd heard too many stories about people hitting a deer at moderate speeds, losing control of the car and killing the whole family. I was going much faster than what anyone might consider moderate. Add that to the fact that most deer dress out around a hundred pounds. This creature had to be well over four hundred pounds on the hoof. The impact would be devastating. The story flashed before my eyes. "Five thousand pound van hits a four hundred pound creature at seventy miles an hour. The force of impact was deadly."

I was speeding towards a rude awaking.

By now the world seemed to be moving in slow motion. My next thought was this had to be a huge buck or a very, very large antelope because he was sporting a dazzling rack of antelope-like horns. Perhaps he was a species from Africa. We were near several private hunting reserves. They stocked exotic animals. Maybe this was something I wasn't familiar with. My mind would not accept that description either. He had majestic antlers, but something was wrong. First of all, he was at least three or four times the size of an Antelope. He was more the size of an elk than an antelope. There was something else. Something about this animal was clearly impossible for me to understand.

Finally, in the super slow motion instant adrenalin gives you, I realized the problem. I saw clearly why my mind was having so much trouble classifying this beast. It was simple really once my mind accepted it. I was having difficulty classifying the beast because he didn't exist. Or rather he couldn't exist. He was a joke. A hoax perpetrated on bumper stickers and post cards throughout the great western United States.

He was absolutely without a doubt an impossibility. And yet there he was, standing in my running lights, real as real gets, immediately in front of me. I was looking at a living breathing absurdity. In that instant of recognition the beast's head turned to the left, so he could stare directly into my eyes as if to say:

"Are you getting this, Tom?"

Then as quickly as he came he left, jumping thirty feet in a bound clearing the highway and disappearing into the trees. It was only then I admitted to myself why his existence was impossible, because he had the body of a giant, six-foot-tall jackrabbit. Thick body, long pink ears, oversized hind jumping or hopping legs, and to eliminate all doubt, a big, fluffy, rabbit's tail. As a finishing touch, he was topped by a fine rack of antelope antlers.

Yes, my friends. That night I saw a real life, honest-to-God, North American Jackalope, half antelope and half jack rabbit. An impossibly large jackrabbit. A creature that does not now nor has ever existed in real life (whatever that is).

WAIT! I Am Absolutely Serious

This is not a joke. I am not pulling your leg. I am not making up a wild Texas tale. This is precisely what I saw. I saw a giant Jackalope that night. I am sharing with you a story, which I believe as true and certain, as my belief the sun will rise in the east tomorrow. Of course, my rational side will agree that this Jackalope belief could be considered impossible.

I've never told this story publicly before for that very reason. Heck, I've never even told my kids, let alone friends and family. I have no desire to be ridiculed or dismissed as someone who is subject to flights into the absurd. I take my credibility very, very seriously. If it weren't for the need to tell this story, I would never have let you in on perhaps my most impossible belief. One that is patently absurd! I can't prove I saw a Jackalope. Everyone in my van was fast asleep except me. I don't have pictures except for the pictures I've seen on post cards in gas stations and those were obvious composites. But I will believe until my dying day that I saw a full-grown giant Jackalope jump/hop in front of my van on a dark mountain highway on a beautiful starlit summer night.

Once we acquire beliefs we tend to hold on to them with a determination and voracity that defies reason. Penelope and I have made it a practice to avoid using the word *belief* or *believe*. Because these words are as deadly as a wagon full of hot, sweating nitroglycerin in an old John Wayne movie. Using those words can open the door to an emotional explosion of catastrophic proportions. Because those words evoke your deepest, most sacred and permanently fixed feelings. Questioning our core beliefs means re-examining our lives. Sometimes, that's exactly what we have to do.

As I drove home that evening all I could think about was why a Jackalope came to me. It was obviously some kind of message, cosmic joke or example of infinite abundance or infinite possibility or whatever. But why a Jackalope? Strangely, I didn't question my sighting. No, that was clear. I saw him plain as day and real as a solid gold Patek Phillippe watch. Yet, he was impossible, so impossible I had no use for it. I hadn't even thought about Jackalopes since I was a child and my family took me to Yellowstone Park. Why had the Universe chosen that night and those circumstances to allow me to see such a modern day, mythical beast? Not something I wanted, thought about or cared about. I was interested in flying saucers. We were less than a hundred miles from Roswell. A flying saucer would have made perfect sense. That I would have understood. Of all the things I could have received, which would prove that infinite possibility is a living breathing reality, I get nonsense. If anything is possible, the Universe could have given me something I really wanted, like a brand new Mercedes free of all charges.

No, I get a living, breathing absurdity. A lunacy. An unmistakable postcard joke. "Welcome to The Land of Enchantment. Watch out for Jackalopes, Tom." Why had he come when I was so alone with my thoughts? Deep thoughts about string theory and the multiverse. Why had he turned to look me in the eyes like he had a message for me? *Are you getting this, Tom?* Why couldn't I let this sighting fade into the shadows of doubt? I wanted to believe my newly found realization that infinite possibility was a tangible, practical and physical reality. But a Jackalope?! What in the world did that prove? I couldn't tell anybody. They'd think I was just telling another joke and laugh me off. Give me something I can use! How about a giant nugget of gold? I was in the mountains all weekend for crying out loud! That would certainly prove the concept of infinite possibility.

I didn't even tell my wife what I had seen for several days. When I did I could see the doubt in her eyes even as she tried to believe what I was telling her was true. I'd seen it before. She was thinking, *you just keep getting weirder and weirder.*

Flash Of Insight

Finally, it hit me, many years later. I was living in California, struggling to sell a screenplay, when the realization hit. I had taken the family to a movie and we were all totally absorbed in the show. I was having fun. It'd been a while since I'd done something strictly for fun. I was relaxed and enjoying my day with the family. I was really enjoying the movie until the ending. It was a cheap copout to convention. I didn't like the ending, but I was incensed by it well beyond what a reaction to a movie as good as *The Commitments* deserves. The ending seemed absurd. It fell back on the old saw that all Irish stories must have a sad ending. I thought it was a joke, an absurd joke. I couldn't let it go and I shared my thoughts, freely. I'm sure my family wanted to kill me by the time we got home. Then in one of those flashes of insight that come to all of us for no apparent reason, I understood the Jackalope story. Often moments of inspiration are like that. They are your inspiration, and they don't need to make sense to anyone else. It doesn't have to make sense. You just make a connection. It's as simple as that.

I realized that infinite possibility does not mean receiving what you expect or desire. On the contrary, a true illustration of infinite possibility must be something beyond what you want or expect. The unexpected can show you a completely different perspective, a different view of the world. The absurd has power because it is unexpected. Shocking. Disturbing. Unsettling. It makes the impossible possible. It pushes your boundaries. Creates paradoxes for your mind to resolve. This stretches your imagination to reach new previously unimagined heights.

Imagination is the artist's blueprint. All great creations are born in the imagination.

Infinite possibility transcends anything that can be easily understood or believed. Anything I believe. Anything you believe. Or anything anyone believes or will ever believe. Because infinite possibility is, after all, infinite and without measure. We are merely finite.

The finite can never fully understand the infinite.

Penelope reminded me that as a child she heard me say many times, "All things are possible. They're just not all probable." Which really means, "All things are not possible because we only believe in what is probable." I had been limiting the concept of infinite possibility all my life. We all do. Clearly, I did not accept the existence of a Jackalope as probable. If something seems improbable, it seems very hard for us to process. So we tend to discount what we experience as improbable and therefore not possible. Our minds then label this event, experience or thing as impossible, and we look for justification in why we mistakenly thought we experienced something we didn't. In truth, we can be mistaken, but not always. Sometimes our finite minds simply don't want to accept the concept of the Infinite.

Here's The Payoff

Once you grasp the vastness, the impossibly enormous, unlimited scope of what is possible, then problems of lack can vanish quicker than the morning fog on a sunny day and be no more.

Now, I harbor no hope or desire that you believe my Jackalope story. It's not yours to believe or disbelieve. It's mine. It was given to me so I could grasp the depth of meaning contained in the concept of infinite possibility. I present it here because it is such an outlandish example of what's possible.

Remember it. Even if you remember it with a smile of skeptical reservation. Remember it next time you are in a dark and lonely place. Next time you are desperately in need of help, guidance, love, protection, justice, truth and peace – healing by any name. Anytime you are tempted by the stress and circumstances of your life to think, "I can't do it. It simply cannot be done. It is impossible."

Remember my Jackalope. Let my absurd lesson serve as a living postcard from the Universe reminding you that nothing is impossible in this life. Because we live in a world of infinite possibility.

Oh, in case you don't know by now, we have a name for lessons like this one. Things that happen that couldn't possibly happen. We call them miracles.

Miracles Happen

The word miracle gets thrown around a lot these days, so let me be specific. I use the term with a degree of wonder and divine respect. I remember the times in my life when I read accounts of stigmata, spontaneous combustion or the successful teleportation of atoms. Each and every one of those phenomena was a miracle. It was impossible and yet it happened. A miracle that encouraged and heartened me. Realizing that something I personally considered impossible had actually occurred caused my mind to wander into a creative and expansive journey of impossible ideas that might just be possible after all. Quantum Selling resulted from just such a mental voyage after I went to a P.K. (psychokinesis) Party and bent spoons using only the power of my mind.

The Jackalope changed forever how I understood what is possible. Miracles are not restricted to ancient text or purely religious matters. Miracles are simply a part of life. Because woven into the fabric of our reality is this perfectly reasonable notion that anything is possible. Without any doubt, absolutely anything in this sensual time zone of consciousness we call reality is possible. Regardless of what common wisdom says, regardless of what you or others think, regardless of whether it seems useful, probable, or even plausible, anything – absolutely anything is possible.

We live in a world of infinite possibility which extends the 'me first' understanding I initially held. Infinite possibility removes all limits. Even the limits we impose on ourselves.

To doubt the power and magnitude of infinite possibility in your own life is to doubt the existence of the Source of All Creation. How limiting and damning it is then to believe only what is safe and acceptable. Limitation is a pernicious lie destroying our health, our economy, our very existence. You are not limited. You live in a world of infinite possibility. And all you have to do to access this miracle is to accept the simple fact that infinite possibility is always with you, awaiting your acceptance.

Now it's time for another miracle. The miracle of my death, rebirth and complete recovery. This miracle is not just for me. This one's for you, too. I died, returned and recovered, all miraculously, so you and I could both expand our understanding of what is possible. So you could experience through me a very brief glimpse of the power of the Glory of the All Glorious. That you might better understand the infinite power you have within you. So you can heal your life and in doing so heal your children and your grandchildren and their children. So you can heal the world little by little and bit by bit.

I can hardly wait myself. I've never allowed myself to go back and examine that experience in detail. I'm sure I'll gain a great deal from it too. First, however, we have to take a brief time out.

I'm taking the day off tomorrow. I hadn't planned it, but these things happen to the best of us. Hey, why don't you join me? We can celebrate together. I think I even hear some music playing. We have all the makings of a party. No need to change clothes. What you're wearing is fine.

CHAPTER 8
Double Double

It was a bright, warm, beautiful morning in paradise. Two red-tailed hawks had made up a nest in the ancient Orangewood tree in my backyard the year before. By all rights, I should have been watching for their return. Instead, I was holed up in my office listening to Robert Johnson sing his blues like nobody before or since, although many have tried. Robert was a poor, itinerant and uneducated musician who wrote 29 songs, every one incredible. Songs like Sweet Home Chicago, Kindhearted Woman, They're Red Hot and The Crossroad Blues, which Eric Clapton turned into a number one hit. Clapton is an amazing guitarist, but when he first heard Robert Johnson's one and only album he was astonished. He couldn't play a single song. Obviously, he learned how. His Me and Mr. Johnson is one of my favorite albums. Many artists from The Rolling Stones to the Red Hot Chili Peppers have made monster hits out of a Robert Johnson song. Still, there is nothing like listening to the master himself.

I'd taken the day off. I was trying to celebrate – perhaps, endure would be more accurate – the fifth anniversary of my demise. You'd think that I'd have been grateful. As friends and family were quick to remind me this was my rebirth day, a day to celebrate coming back to life. I suppose they were right, but

I didn't seem to have the same visceral reaction to coming back as I did to losing everything I ever had. You know what they say, "If you have your health, you have everything." Well, I didn't have my whole health anymore, and I couldn't seem to shake that dreadful feeling of all I had lost. *Lack reaches into your heart and sucks infinity completely out of your soul.* I couldn't see or imagine one single good thing to come from my experience.

That's how scarcity consciousness works. You get caught up in what you don't have and the good things in your life seem to blur and fade into a gray nothingness. They run and hide for fear you get happy again. You start to feel like nothing you will ever do will have a snowball's chance in hell of turning out for the better. The funny thing is all you really have to do is think of one good thing in your life and everything will change instantly. Now that can take some doing. Scarcity consciousness is a stubborn little troublemaker. He holds on tight telling you, "Forget your dreams, Loser. Nothing good is coming your way anytime soon. Time to accept the awful truth. Deal with it!" That day I couldn't for the life of me think of anything good in my life.

I was feeling sorry for myself. Maybe I felt like I had earned the right. After all I was still crippled up, five years later. Where is my full and complete recovery? All I could think about was never being able to do the things I did before my stroke. Maybe I was still mad at God. I told myself He did this to me. He was to blame. Let Him deal with a crippled and ruined servant, the heck with writing a book. I didn't have anything worth saying anyway. Besides everything I write comes out like garbage. I'm no good. I'm worthless. *Whaaaa!*

Heavens above! All that self-pity makes me sick just to think about it now. We all face times when we feel inadequate, not up to the challenge in front of us, but that is just an illusion, a scarcity consciousness interpretation of the situation. We never face a task in which we are inadequate. We may need help, but as they say at Hogwarts, help is always given to those who ask. It's the Law of Attraction. You attract what you need when you need it. The best way to handle a bout with scarcity consciousness is to do the Texas Side Step. Simply put, move out of the way. Change directions. Do something fun. Put a little joy in your heart.

I was to trying with all my might to write something light, as Diane had suggested, but it wasn't working out for me. So I did the only logical thing I could do. Rather than think about my experience another minute, I snuck out the back door, eschewing Diane's healthy homemade lunch for a Double Double, fries and a Diet Coke.

If you're not from California, a Double Double is the world's best cheeseburger. It's two patties of fresh beef, never frozen, and two slices of American cheese with a thick slice of onion, lettuce, tomatoes, pickles and a very good sauce. The fries are made from potatoes cut fresh daily. All prepared hot and greasy at the one and only In-N-Out Burger. It is my *Cheeseburger in Paradise.* Eat your heart out, Jimmy Buffett.

It didn't matter that such fast food lunches may have been one of the reasons I had a stroke in the first place. I had to have one this day of all days. When I was sitting in my room in Acute Rehab watching spring emerge from a particularly cold winter (by So Cal standards) I had one constant desire. Every day I would imagine myself sitting outside that very restaurant eating a Double Double, fries and a Diet Coke. I don't remember if I had the same meal the year before, but chances are I did. I bet Robert Johnson would have chased his blues away with a Double, Double if he'd have had the chance.

After lunch, I thought about my first full day in ICU. I had already had all seven strokes and the diagnosis was in. The doctors had already declared that I was going to spend the rest of my life in bed. They declared that I would never walk, talk, feed, dress myself, or horror of all horrors, watch TV again.

Basically, the doctors had decided that I was screwed. And their decision alone would have guaranteed my fate. I would never have been evaluated for Acute Rehab if their diagnosis had stood. Their prophecy would have become self-fulfilling.

Diane and Penelope, however, intervened. They threw a massive fit. Our family has never been big believers in that whole god-complex thing. You know, medical doctors believing they are the repositories of all knowledge. So my ladies challenged the diagnosis, vociferously.

I had already made that hurried trip across the hospital to the CAT scan unit seven times, one after each incident. The doctors claimed the CAT scans made the situation perfectly clear. My last two strokes were on the brainstem. That meant I was a vegetable, and I could not possibly recover. Which I knew was not true because I was promised a full and complete recovery if I chose to return and do my work. But nobody was listening to me. Later Diane told me I was making mostly gurgling sounds, not real words. Probably the reason I wasn't consulted.

Thank God, my women do not take "hell, no" for an answer. They were my Angels of Possibility. They saved me. I could hear Diane in the hall clamoring for an MRI. She was the loudest. She and Penelope demanded that they prove their diagnosis with an MRI. Of course, the doctors didn't need one. They were satisfied with the CAT scans. Penelope was contending they didn't know her father's will to win, and threatening to move me to a better hospital and tell the world about it. Diane was demanding at least a chance at recovery starting with an MRI. The pressure was constant. Boy, that's one conversation I would have loved to have on video.

See, if you don't start rehabilitation immediately, the brain never starts to develop new neural pathways. You must start forcing your body to work as soon as possible after the stroke or your recovery is finished before it has a chance to start. And these self-anointed medical gods were recommending I be sent to long-term recovery, which is really twenty years of bed rest.

I had the MRI late that day. Since the MRI machine was in a separate building about 100 yards from the Emergency Room exit they were required to transport me by ambulance. As a protection from something, I never knew what, they refused to let me have any water. My throat was so dry I thought it would permanently fuse shut. First I had to wait on my bed by the emergency door until the ambulance showed up. There was some hold up. Man, did I need water. Naturally, there was an hour's wait once we drove the full 100 yards. That way my throat could dry out a little more. A kind, young nurse did give me a few chips of ice to suck. When my turn finally came, the MRI machine was old and small. It smelled of sweat, fear and disinfectant. The technician secured my head in a fixed position then asked if I'd like to listen to music. I gave her a thumbs up on classical.

Inside the MRI it was hot and tight. I couldn't move my head, I could barely swallow, and I was in there the better part of an hour listening to a scratchy and wavering rendition of some blasted requiem. A requiem, for crying out loud! Who would even use that in a hospital? They put me in a hot, stinking, coffin-sized hole listening to a requiem that seemed itself to be dying! "Would this be my swan song? Would these be the sounds and smells I took to my grave? Could I please get just one stupid sip of water?!" That's what consumed my thoughts during my fifty-seven minutes inside the machine. I knew it wasn't so. I knew I wasn't dying again. I knew I had a job to do. But still, I am surprised I didn't have yet another stroke right there.

Should have opted for country.

Fortunately, I lived. The MRI proved my angels correct. The strokes were near, but not exactly on the brainstem. I don't think the doctors were entirely convinced. Sarcastically, the neurosurgeon said, "Well, either the CAT Scans were wrong or somehow the stroke event in Tom's brain has moved, because it was on the brainstem."

On my second day in ICU the head of physical therapy came into my room for what I imagine was intended as an exercise in placating the family. She brought with her a strange looking device, which she stood next to the bed while she "evaluated" me. The device had pads where you placed your knees and handles for pulling yourself up into an upright position. Her decision would now determine if I was headed to the Acute Rehab unit or off to Sleepy Acres.

She was pleasant enough, but she ended her little talk by saying, "If you can someday pull yourself up on this machine, then you'll be ready for rehab. We can try it when you're feeling stronger." Someday she'd let me try. Someday! Not that day, of course, because she wasn't even giving me the chance to try.

She predetermined my evaluation without letting me try to pull myself up. She was writing me off as a lost cause. And why not? The doctors' living-death-by-bed-rest diagnosis was right there on the chart in front of her? She turned and started selling the long-term recovery program to Diane and Penelope.

I didn't listen. Because a very loud voice in my head told me in no uncertain words:

> "Tom, get up on that device immediately. Now! This is your one and only chance."

I pushed with a strength I didn't feel and muscles I didn't have five minutes earlier. I clawed at the bed covers. I strained, sweated and pushed with everything I had. I ignored the therapist who was now trying to keep me down lest I hurt myself. I was determined because I've learned to listen to those voices in my head. I've spent many hours in the Portal using our Quantum Selling techniques. Nothing was going to keep me from this tryout.

Penelope yelled at the technician and the nurse who'd joined her in the restraint efforts. Both my women were saying, "Give him a chance!" Eventually they did.

I managed to pull the IV loose in my right arm, but I didn't care. I had a job to do. I pulled, dragged and some how willed my paralyzed body up on that blasted contraption. I turned to look at the technician, smiled out the left side of my face (the right side remember was totally paralyzed), and just hung there. I then fell back on the bed exhausted.

Diane told me later the therapist said in an almost inaudible voice, "Well, maybe he can make it."

I couldn't hear a thing, because the loose IV was now dripping potassium directly under my skin. It burned like hell's fire incarnate. I struggled with the limited strength I had left to pull it out. The nurse was apparently convinced that I had flipped out and once again came to my unneeded assistance, trying to keep me from stopping the terrible burning IV. It turns out it was against hospital policy to remove the IV without first attaching a new one. Even if the thing is doing you harm. I explained the situation very clearly. At least, I thought I did. Unfortunately, what came out sounded a little more like, "Gurlsh dchrung chingh blurching muddr flushling arm."

Nobody listens to me.

The technician was already gone, so the nurse tried to enlist my protectors in her restraint efforts. They knew better. So she rushed off to get help. A good thing really, because I was going to bite her if she tried to stop me one more time. That probably would have earned me physical restraints. When she came back with the charge nurse I had the IV out of my arm and dripping on the floor. The charge nurse looked at the bright red patch on my arm and told the defender of hospital rules, "This looks like a burn. Get him a Tylenol as soon as you get a new IV started."

So much for thinking outside the box.

I felt like I'd taken one small step forward, but wondered if I'd ever make it out of that place alive, so I could have my full and complete recovery. While I lay there completely exhausted, I saw the look of pride on my wife's face. That look gave me the strength I needed for the coming month. I think Penelope was looking for the physical therapist, so she could close the deal and get me into the rehab unit.

In the quiet hours after my defenders went home and the night crew came on, I lay wide-awake thinking. Man, I did a lot of thinking. At night the ICU is relatively quiet. All I could hear was the steady electronic beat of the monitors. The steady crinkle and whoosh of the plastic leg squeezers chasing away blood clots. And there was always the hurried rush and sense of dread and anxiety that accompanied a Code Blue announcement on the overhead speakers. Always a constant reminder that ICU is a dangerous place to be. Of course, there were the awful, ever present hospital odors. Even the food started to absorb that smell. I was only getting Jell-O, so the effect was minimal. I tried in those hours to process what was happening to me. My emotions were really a mess.

Yes, I did a lot of thinking.

Now, thinking can be very dangerous. Especially when you are still grieving the loss of the life you had. I was so depressed. All I could think about was loss. I couldn't cry and I couldn't forgive. That would come later. Denial was impossible because I was reminded constantly of my condition. And I sure couldn't make a deal with the Generous One I blamed for doing this to me. So I was angry. I thought and I fumed.

But I knew as well as I knew my own name that I had received a promise of a full and complete recovery during my second death experience. I knew something nobody else knew. I knew it with unquestioned certainty. It gave me undying confidence. I was guaranteed a full and complete recovery in the Presence of the Generous One! And that guarantee was absolute. That one piece of knowledge gave me great hope. That hope sustained me through my darkest hours and most difficult tests. I believe I was given this absolute knowing as a gift and a reminder of the power of my connection, my oneness with the Infinite. It was a constant reminder that through God, we have the power to move mountains.

What was the extent of my Miracle Healing? I knew that the sixth stroke was on my brain stem, exactly as the doctors had explained. The fact that the MRI clearly showed that the stoke event was *not* on my brain stem was not correcting a mistake caused by the CAT scans. It was proof to me that the location of the damage caused by the stroke had moved. It was originally on my brain stem, but when I chose to come back and complete my mission, the damaged area moved. It's not a very likely or probable explanation, but it was possible and that was enough.

The catastrophic damage inside my brain moved.

Crazy, I know. Such a thing could not happen in the physical world. The stroke is where the stroke is. Period. Saying it moved is as crazy as seeing a real life four hundred pound Jackalope.

Of course, that is no crazier than reading a book by a man who died twice, getting better with the second experience.

Know Yourself First

I know I need to get into the details of my death experience, which I promise to do as soon as you know some important information about who you are. See, that's the key to everything. You must know who you are. You can't go through life without knowing who you are; not if you want the gift I brought back for you. It would not mean nearly as much – no, it's more than that – this amazing gift wouldn't have the same healing, life changing, world changing impact if you didn't know who you are. You couldn't receive the abundance of monumental Good waiting for you, right now. Good that will lift you above the mundane distractions of this temporal plain to a heightened and powerful perspective. Knowing who you are is absolutely essential! I wouldn't be doing my job if I didn't give you a few hints and clues.

What do you say we take a look? Maybe we can throw some light on that big question for you. The one you absolutely must answer if we truly want to fill your life with Miracle Healing. You want that, right? You want to fulfill your purpose for coming to earth at this time and in this place, right? You want to eliminate your scarcity consciousness once and for all, right? Certainly, you want to realize those deep and persistent desires that tell you there is something more waiting for you, something better? Of course you do. All it takes is the answer to one simple question. You know the one.

Who Am I?

CHAPTER 9

The Chosen One

The other day a friend, Paul, told me how much he respected me for never complaining about my constant pain. I honestly had to think what he was talking about. Then it hit me, the searing pain in my right hip and the stabbing pain in my right shoulder cause me to tighten up and grimace occasionally. Perhaps, less occasionally than I thought. I had to think, because in my experience that pain is really inconsequential. I don't like it. I'd rather I didn't have it, but that's where I am. I would rather focus on my recovery, which is going well. Pain is relative. Hey, I'm alive and walking around, writing, watching TV and everything. What's a little pain compared to all that?

It's amazing how quickly my really severe pain vanished in the ER. All pain, not just the physical pain I was suffering at the time. Also the emotional pain and mental anguish I'd been suffering for most of my life. It all vanished in the blink of an eye. It really underlines for me the fact that pain is a figment of our imagination – albeit a persistent one, of course. When I think about it, one minute I was joking with Penelope and having my picture taken, enduring some really unbearable pain, then I was looking down at a room full of doctors and nurses, good people all, working with the precision of a finely tuned race car. In that instant of realization, I was gone and the only thing I felt was curiosity. It was a beautiful thing to experience and now ponder. The pain seemed insignificant, more of a distraction than anything. In the moment pain can be frightening, troublesome, foreboding and even debilitating, but one way or another it eventually ends and is no more.

The time has come for me to share my first death experience with you and the rest of the world. Part of me wants to put it off a little longer because I must re-live it all again to convey the true and honest version. I've tried this several times already. Not in written form, but verbally. I told my psychologist once. I tried to talk about it in my group meetings twice, and to Penelope once. Her reaction was the best. Probably that's why she has been pushing me so hard to let it out. The trouble was, I hadn't processed it yet. This is a natural reaction when processing the awesome truth of facing an experience, which you remember as painful. The more painful, the harder it is to face. In case you don't already know, facing your issues head on is the only way you can truly heal. You, me, anyone. You have to re-live the situation to let go of it; otherwise you'll stay stuck in that pain and that time frame.

If you don't face your pain and process your experience, you won't get the chance to recognize what you may have gained. Until then, all you remember is what you lost. As Einstein first demonstrated, you cannot lose matter, which, of course, is energy. If something is lost, then something else is gained. If you burn a wooden log you gain smoke, moisture and heat. Nothing is ever lost. The same is true of us humans. I have lost my ability to run and jump, so I must have gained something else. Facing your pain, facing the challenges in your life with integrity, living every single moment authentically is like going on a treasure hunt. You must process the past so you can find the nuggets of gold, the raw gems waiting in every test and difficulty.

This takes you to a higher level of consciousness. It elevates your being one more step toward a truly transcendent version of you. If you don't face your experiences in absolute honesty, then you will stumble though a hardscrabble life full of troubles and pain that will at times befuddle your understanding. You start to feel that God hates you, or the world is against you. Nothing seems to go right. The very talents you have come to recognize and depend upon fail you. All because you missed a lesson you needed to learn. Or you turned left when you needed to turn right. You denied the truth that was given to you because you were so stuck in loss and pain you couldn't see the benefit. You missed the gold because you were focused on the blisters that came from digging. You must learn the lessons that come from facing your pain so you can process it all and move on.

Release Your Pain

Denial will cause you mountains of pain and difficulty, because it will take away your infinite healing possibilities. If you deny the severity of the difficulties in your life, whether they are physical, material or emotional then you are living a lie. You cannot say, "tweedle dee" and start spouting affirmations and think you are fixing a darn thing. You can't start a new business or take a new spouse or go to a new doctor and escape the troubles coming your way because those troubles are not an end in themselves. They are merely guideposts screaming *TURN AROUND AND RELEASE YOUR PAIN!* When you seal your injury deep inside yourself, hiding that hurting part of you, it injures and retards your consciousness. When you do that there is nothing all the power and might of the Universe can do to help you, except to give you more pain in an attempt to get you to turn around and face the real cause of all the trouble. All because you are not allowing yourself to admit anything is wrong. You are requiring your consciousness to lie for you. To deny your injury, you are denying yourself the opportunity to grow and expand, which is your ultimate reason for being here. Would you deny the pain of a heart attack? Probably not; it's too severe. Besides, you know you cannot fix that by yourself. What about the crippling pain of economic difficulties, or a troubled marriage? Would you just push ahead without facing the real cause of that pain? Would you deny your own culpability and blame your troubles on someone or something else, washing your hands of all responsibility? "It's my wife's fault. It's the boss' fault. It's the competition's fault. It's the government's fault. It's the economy's fault." Or would you stop and act with courage, maturity and integrity? Take responsibility for your own actions; face the tough music of righting any wrongs you may have caused and moving forward with a clear head and conscience.

Maybe the Universe is telling you that your path has changed, but you don't want to believe it. That's too painful to consider. You'd have to face new challenges, new tests, new difficulties. They are, for heaven's sakes – new! How frightening that can be. You'd have to grow to meet and overcome new challenges. It's always easier to do what's comfortable, what we're used to doing, what you're doing now. Why face new challenges and new tests, when it's so much easier to take the same tests you've already experienced?

Because you are not growing and expanding, that's why.

Nobody said this life is easy. When you deny the test right in front of you, you are stagnating. Stagnation leads to certain death. You are here to grow and expand. If you are not doing that, you are not needed anymore. Growing and expanding is the whole point of this life. Once a plant stops growing it starts to die. It has outlived its usefulness. The only thing left for it is to become fertilizer for new life. You are no different. You cannot grow and expand taking last year's tests. Denial of the truth, refusing to face your pain wreaks havoc with your life. It creates more pain that you ever need to face. All because you are not following your path with courage and integrity. You must be brutally honest with yourself and face your challenges with a courage that comes from knowing your main responsibility to yourself is to grow and learn.

The First Talisman Of Healing

That doesn't mean you have to give up who you are. I am at heart a salesman. Some people think salesmen are basically dishonest. I disagree. A good salesman never lies. The truth is so much more powerful. When I'm selling I get excited about the benefits of whatever product or service I am suggesting. I point out the features and benefits and overcome any concerns someone may have because that's who I am. That's my job! I love selling. I love seeing and hearing from folks who benefit from what I sell. I remember a man who bought a life insurance policy from me, who was so afraid to waste money on a separate policy on his wife. He was the breadwinner after all. I suggested that he, at least, put a small rider on his policy for her. He did, reluctantly. Five years later I ran into him. He jumped up from his table in a restaurant and ran over as I came in the door. He hugged me and thanked me for that rider. Turns out his wife suffered a massive stoke and died at forty-four. He said that if he hadn't had that little rider on her he couldn't have paid the bills and would have gone bankrupt. Knowing I helped ease his pain was awesome! Knowing I helped folks get over the hurdles that were keeping them from their success gives me great satisfaction. If I didn't believe in the product, then I wouldn't sell it. I believe selling is perhaps the greatest profession on earth (next to being a parent). I'm never going to change that. I have many defects, which I can change, but I am always going to be who I am. Clearing my human defects requires that I have the courage to be honest with myself. I cannot pretend I am something I am not. I cannot do that for money or love. All I can hope to do is become the best version of me I can.

This is the elevated version of me.

Having the courage to be honest with yourself is the mark of an elevated human. Because once you are honest with yourself nothing can hold you back. You can become the best possible version of you. The person you came here to become. Remember you are safe and protected at all times and under all conditions. When you have a problem, give it to God. Let Him do the heavy lifting. All you need to do is what's in front of you every day.

Plan, yes. Execute, yes. Worry, never.

Your Miracle Too

I am going to reveal all the details of my experience, but first I need to point out a few things. First and foremost, this Miracle is not just for me. This impossible, yet very real story – this

Miracle – is for you. It is your miracle, too. It was given to me, so I could grow, overcome my fear and doubt and purge my heart of centuries of immaturity and "stinking thinking," as Zig Ziegler would say. Unknown to me, I had some issues that needed fixing before I could succeed. It took the stroke to open the doors to my complete recovery. As much as I wanted my full and complete recovery to be about regaining my physical prowess, it was about so much more. It was given to me because I had the skills and background to sell it to you. This miracle is really your miracle.

I was given a mission. I've been preparing for this mission my whole life. And my healing makes that mission possible. My talents and the difficulties I've had to overcome have made me the one and only person on this planet who can do what I have been asked to do. Like Harry Potter, I am the Chosen One. Also, like Harry I had to die before I could shed myself of the unseen struggle I held deep within. The hero's journey again.

If that sounds pretentious to you, join the club. In my weaker moments, I feel like I'm overstepping my role. Wearing the robes of those who are far better equipped and more deserving than me. Admitting that I am the Chosen One was big for me. That means completing my mission is my responsibility. I can't expect Penelope or anyone else to do the work that's for me to do. I am here on this planet in this time frame to do what I do best. No one else can do it. Sure, my human side wants to have this responsibility pass to someone else, but it doesn't work that way. God gave me the talents, the second chance, and then reaffirmed my mission in rather dramatic fashion, as you'll see soon. Who am I to question God? He is the All-Knowing, the Omnipotent.

You Are The Chosen One

You are as much the Chosen One as I am. You have a different job, but you were chosen. You were chosen above all the countless souls in the infinite sea of souls to live in this consciousness time zone. Your Light was chosen to come into this world at the exact moment, place and parentage of your birth. You were given the exact talents, abilities and experiences you have so you could do what it is you were given to do. Even your defects, tests and difficulties were given to you specifically, so that you could overcome them and become a stronger, better version of yourself. Maybe you are filled with self-doubt or poor self-esteem and think your life is worthless and without consequence. Maybe you suffer from an abundance of false modesty and feel this praise is unjustified. Maybe you are afraid of accepting the high level of your own station. Maybe you're suffering from the reverse and you think you are above all the claptrap of our modern culture. Maybe you think you are not responsible for anyone else. Maybe you think you are very special and filled with such powerful talents you cannot be bothered by such trivial nonsense. Maybe you think that you are not special in any way, that this whole Chosen One thing is just too far from what you have been taught to accept, any of it.

You absolutely have another think coming!

I've seen what you can do. It was real. You were purely amazing. You acted with such courage and grace that I was awestruck at the sight. My whole essence beamed with pride at what you accomplished. Watching you stand and face the onslaught of all the forces pitted against you and all that you love was the most beautiful thing I have ever seen.

What onslaught? Which forces? When and where? I know you still have no idea what I'm referring to. Hang in there. Relax your desire to have everything spoon-fed in some antiquated top down lecture. Go with the flow. Suspend your control and disbelief for a little while and open yourself to the mystery. The fact is you really know more than you think you do.

Here is another fact: Accepting your station as Chosen One is essential to your growth and expansion. Most of your denial or obfuscation can be attributed to ego. You think you know better than your higher power. Regardless of what you think, feel or believe, you are unique among all humankind living or dead. There is no one exactly like you ever to live on this earth. Yes, you are special and no, you are not more or less important than anyone else. What you must realize is that only you can do what you do exactly as you do it. You have been chosen because you are you. Only you can do your part in advancing the inevitable and long awaited maturity of humankind. Using the talents you have been given is your responsibility for having the chance to live here now. This is the price you pay for all the wonderful things this world has to offer. All the things you can have merely for the asking.

You are the Chosen One of God. No question about it. But you knew that, didn't you? Deep inside. You have always known that you were here for a reason, for a purpose that you were meant to do great things. That you could contribute in some way. Maybe you just didn't know what you were supposed to do. What the big picture was.

You must, however, decide for yourself who you are. That's the way it works. You have the right and responsibility to accept the mantle offered to you. Or refuse it. Only you can decide.

A Garden of Paradise awaits you. Abundance beyond imagination, the bounty of all Creation is flowing to you, surrounding you and embracing you effortlessly, instantly. Peace, love and the joy your soul has craved for millennia. Of this garden Sir Abdu'l-Baha, early leader of the Baha'i Faith and son of the Prophet founder Baha'u'llah said, "At the gate of the garden, some stand and look within, but do not care to enter. Others step inside, behold its beauty, but do not penetrate far. Still others encircle the garden, inhaling the fragrance of the flowers; and having enjoyed its full beauty, pass out again by the same gate. But there are always some who enter, and becoming intoxicated with the splendor of what they behold remain for life to tend the garden."

They stay because they know who they are.

Me? I know who I am. I'm a gardener. I'm the Chosen One. A traveler to that undiscovered country, a humbled guru and salesman, who returned with a gift of Miracle Healing. I am the One given a miracle life and a mission to do his part to enlist your help in elevating yourself, those you love and humankind as a whole.

How about you? You have already stopped to enter and inhaled the fragrance of the garden. Will you stay to tend the garden? Or will you eventually pass out again? Who are you? This is something only you can decide. Only you can decide who you are.

Time to do what I do. Tell my story. Your story. Our story.

Come back with me as my consciousness hovers above my mortal body in Saddleback Hospital, March 28th, 2009, sometime in the early afternoon.

CHAPTER 10

Arc Of Light

The trumpeting call of the doctors' orders, the hurried rush of my children leaving the room, the frenetic cadence of the attending nurses set against the mechanical syncopation of the ER machines, all these urgent and quickly orchestrated noises became my swan song. This was my requiem. The last thing I felt while inside my body was the electrical harness as it was glued tightly to my chest. But honestly, I only vaguely remember it. The crushing pain in my heart combined with the unrelenting, stabbing pain of my body contracting on itself took center stage. If I had been able to catch a breath, I would have screamed to the highest reaches of heaven for relief.

Immediately, the sounds and the pain were gone, fading into the most delicious silence I've ever known. I was disoriented for a brief moment. Quickly, I realized that I was no longer part of the drama below. Only my body was. I was looking down from above. I could see my body lying dead still in the hospital bed as a half dozen men and women labored over me. It was a me that wasn't me anymore and a body that I didn't need. It all seemed curious to me then. Certainly, it was nothing of great concern, just another past life. The doctors and nurses were injecting fluids. Pushing buttons. Checking monitors. The entire drama fading slowly to black as I watched. I was completely at peace for the first time I can remember in this human experience. I was at peace with myself. All the worldly trials and difficulties, the worries and frustrations I was so accustomed to suffering had become less than nothing. They simply did not exist.

For the briefest instant, I was surrounded by a warm, loving and welcoming darkness. It was not frightening or full of threat and pain, as I had once imagined. It was simply safe. It was like coming home from college for the holidays to my parents' house. The house was dark, but I was home. I was completely safe and protected. Nothing could harm me in any way, ever again.

As I lost interest in my past life, the images of the continuing drama below faded. Without hesitation I turned to go on. This part is tricky because it's hard to translate what I experienced by using the limited mundane vocabulary and knowledge base of this world. I felt like I was "looking up" which is strange enough since I knew I was not in my body. It was lying on a bed in Saddleback Hospital emergency room. Still, I felt like I was looking up, the opposite direction from whence I came. I was looking up because I was drawn by the sound of an indescribably brilliant and unavoidably compelling, expanding and descending point of Pure White Light. Yes, I was drawn by the sound of the Light. An amazing sound or song – to me it was angel or spirit music. I don't know how else to explain it. It made me feel elevated, joyous and confident. It called to me like what I might imagine as the call of a divine siren. I can't explain the music of the Light other than to say it was heavenly and more beautiful than anything I had ever known or imagined.

The Light was the main attraction. The Light was beyond this world. It was closer to a living, breathing Supreme form than a beam of light, as we know it. It was both alive as a being and as brimming with life as an ocean. It had density, definition and coherence as it extended graciously for me from above like a supercharged greeting of a long awaited welcome. It makes me feel almost giddy today when I think about it. Like a six-year-old watching his mom decorating the house for his seventh birthday.

This Living Light could barely restrain its excitement over my return. What it looked like descending is particularly hard to explain. I still see its brilliance penetrating the delicious darkness all around me, rushing forward, practically leaping with joy. It came from above and grew larger as it came closer as you might expect for an object coming from a great distance smaller at the top and growing larger on the end coming my way. The thing that is difficult to describe is the head or bridge of this massive swooping rescue ship of Light. The driving force was greater in circumference than the column by a comfortable margin larger, but not too large. It looked like an expanded cluster of waves of light energy. The billowing waves of Light seemed to never break, similar to the close up videos of the sun without the feeling of heat, eruptions or danger of any kind. These waves of light energy were in a constant state of rolling, ever-cresting motion, infinitely deep.

The closer the bridge came, the deeper and higher it seemed until I could not detect its beginning or its ending. This living, rolling collar of light appeared to be generating the elongated, billowy column of white light in its wake.

When I think back I remember it smelled and felt "wonderful" as in full of wonder as well as a wonder to behold. It was an ocean of wonder and beauty coming just for me – just for me! I was thrilled beyond anything words can describe. I have always felt like a failure. No matter how hard I worked and how much I accomplished sooner or later all my efforts seemed destined to amount to a good try. And I'd be left for all to see a failure standing in the emperor's new clothes. But this overwhelmingly joyous welcome was in my honor. The highest honor I could ever imagine. I will never forget the Light's overwhelmingly happy and inclusive personality. Like it had been waiting to celebrate my return for centuries. I cannot explain why I thought centuries, but I did. I was so excited and awed.

When I try to describe the shape and texture of the Arc what I get is a well defined, and constantly rolling cloud. Like an impossibly thick and infinitely intelligent billowing cloud floating high above the Nebraska prairie on a beautiful, quiet summer day. Only this cloudlike form unfolded for me in a fast rolling welcome which reminded me of Diane early in our marriage, running to greet me from a returning airplane trip. Two lovers for whom separation was the ultimate death and reunion was life itself. The White Light was overjoyed to see and embrace me, to welcome me home. I knew we were one and inseparable before, since and forever. Then it wrapped around me and through me until everything was Light. Divine Unity. And yet at the same time I could see the column of Light ascending upwards perhaps a gift of infinite perspective. It was as though I could be inside the Light and outside simultaneously which seemed unremarkable at the time.

Infinitely Bright

This Living Light shone with a brilliance greater than a quadrillion suns. Although its brilliance was attractive, not harsh and burning the way the sun is. It illuminated everything within me and outside me. It was brilliant in the way it held all that is, all colors, all sounds, all possibilities, all realities, all at once. It was so much more than an infinitely brilliant light. It was an Arc of Light sent by the Supreme Source of All Wisdom, Knowledge and Beauty.

To call the Arc a sentient being would be an insult to the glory and majesty that surrounded and penetrated my essence. This magnificent Form was beyond my understanding of consciousness. It radiated such an abundance of kindness, understanding and love that I kept my interest bowed in the deepest, most sincere respect. As I recognized this form for what it was I grew afraid. I felt my focus pressured downward, bowed like a suppliant awaiting his verdict from an unimpeachable judge. I was filled with the apprehension of the poverty of my station and fewness of my attributes. I was standing at the doorway to the eternal. Waiting to meet Him to whom I have forever turned in my times of need. The inadequacies of my soul exposed for all to see, especially me.

All this I experienced by mere exposure to the Light. Never once was I threatened except by my own self-judgment. I had been called by the most powerful invitation and given a welcoming pass to openly seek answers to all the burning questions I desired from the Source of All-Knowledge.

The Arc of Light that was surrounding, encompassing and filling me was more than compelling. It was the essence of life itself. I knew it came from above me, but I don't know if that distinction was a metaphorical or a physical distinction, prob-ably both at the same time. There's one thing that struck me in my first millisecond of observation. Maybe it was an answer to some unspoken question I don't remember now. What struck me was that every word, every sentence, every thought, had, at least, a thousand meanings. Why I focused on words, thoughts and sentences eludes me. Maybe it was because they had always been important to me. Maybe it was because there was so much more to experience than my mind could contain and I was still processing with mundane references. And I searched for the words, sentences and thoughts to understand this experience. Or maybe because that was simply my first question of which I had so many. I don't really know.

It is so difficult to draw this encounter back into my mind because I am forced to process what is an infinite experience with a finite human brain. That's not really possible. The finite can never understand, much less explain, the infinite.

Still I'm required to try. Bear with me.

I felt like I was an invisible biosatellite, like one of those spheres you sometimes unintentionally capture on photographs. Penelope and I know them as travelers. I couldn't see myself, but I was there moving at will. The instant I was attracted to something I was there. My interest was all I needed for trans-portation. No hesitation. No delay. No doubt I was missing out. I was like a child moving and exploring as my interest led me. Those thoughts fill my mind when I reach back into my mem-ory and connect to that experience. I don't question any of it. I can't. I just smile and enjoy.

I came to understand I was in an antechamber, a processing area from which complete access to All-Knowledge is limited. I say came to understand because this knowing was not immediate. Maybe it was immediate; I don't really know. Maybe it just took me some time to remember everything. Like I said, it's hard to explain using the limitations imposed by our words and incredibly restricted knowledge base. It was like walking through a mystical gallery filled with the finest masterpieces of Edouard Manet, Gustav Klimt, Edgar Degas, Van Gough, Picasso, Rivera, Monet, Chagall, Rothko, Georgia O'Keefe, Frida Kahlo; each a symphony of creativity and possibility. Wherever I turned my interest I was overwhelmed with the essence of their power and beauty washing over my being as the visions in the Light swept my soul into a sea of wonder and eternal delight. I was so overwhelmed and consumed by the beauty I was seeing in the Arc of Light, I couldn't imagine a better experience. Nor could I readily process everything I experienced instantly, and certainly not now.

Isn't that the way it is here on earth? When you are in love you can't imagine anything better and yet you are hard pressed to explain why you were in love other than you were. Still, I came to realize that this was only an appetizer. A mere taste of what was to come in an infinitesimally brief glimpse of Paradise.

I was purposely shielded from the glorious experience farther above because I had a decision to make before being allowed beyond. I remember knowing this was not some sort of screening room for good over bad, reward versus punishment. I knew without a doubt that the destination from here was so wonderful and beyond description that no one would or could ever choose to return from it. This was the place for decisions.

That's when I realized dying was my decision.

Home Sweet Forever

After realizing I would make the final decision of whether to live or die I noticed that the Light tasted sweet and inviting. Sweet in every possible way you can imagine. Sweet with excitement, satisfaction, realization, fulfillment, gratification, joy and wonder, yet, at the same time my mouth (which I didn't have, of course) exploded with an amazing, delightful sweetness. Sweeter and cleaner and without any of the unwanted aftertaste or feeling of harm I get from sugar or artificial sweetener. More like the ripest and most delicious Georgia peach imaginable times a trillion. At the time I felt like the Light itself tasted much sweeter than the color purple. Which makes no sense at all until you understand the color purple inside The Light, the one that I'm talking about, was nothing like the purple we know. For every color we see on earth there were a thousand, a trillion – infinite variations inside the Arc of Living Light. Imagine infinite variations of purple. All vibrating with different shades, tints, shapes, textures, flavors, sweet, savory, inviting, expanding, reducing, engaging, inspiring, each with its own particular aroma – there was no beginning and no end. It's unbelievably exhausting trying to explain in human terms what I experienced in the Arc, instantaneously. I'm only trying to convey one tiny fragment of the whole experience. Imagine each infinite variation of the color purple being as infinite as the image of those seven point five billion trillion stars above the mountains in New Mexico.

Imagine yourself looking up at all those stars, planets and nebula, then zoom in so those images are larger and more distinct, each unique, univocal unto itself. This is your vision, your mind can and will do anything you ask it to. Then imagine those celestial images are all purple, each completely different than all the other billion of trillions of star images. Different in shape, texture, intensity, shade, tint, feel. Of course, you must include varieties of purple you have never before seen – never could have seen. Imagine each of the various heavenly images is alive and singing a marvelously compelling song to you while you delight in the fragrance of its unique, enticing and stimulating aroma. One might remind you of home with beef fat and garlic sizzling in a pan in preparation of beef stew while Bob Dylan sings *Tangled Up In Blue* in anticipation of the family arriving. Another the intoxication of Chanel, love and the taste of fresh baked bread with fragrant cheese while Bizet's Carmen plays softly in the moonlight at the outdoor Bistro across from the Eiffel Tower on your honeymoon. The smells, the textures, the tastes, the sounds, the feelings I was experiencing were all imbedded and one, inseparable with each color. Imagine an infinity of this impossibly vast sensual symphony of the color purple. Now, imagine that image only scratches the surface of what I experienced. Here in this earthly experience, that kind of thinking boggles the mind until you dismiss the possibilities as too much to think about, too much to process. More than our finite minds could ever begin to conceive. There in the Arc it was as natural as relaxing by a babbling brook.

Numbers were absurd. Numbering anything was again like trying to count those billions of trillions of stars because everything existed within The Arc of Light. Everything! Everything that is, was, or ever could possibly exist, even the most unimaginable variations of the most inconceivable possibilities. My Jackalope was there. Probably, because it was my most impossible belief and I was looking for him. At first he appeared exactly as I saw him on that mountain road spotlighted in my running lights, jumping quickly across the highway into the pitch-blackness of the forest. I remember thinking, "slow down!" as he turned to look at me. *Are you getting this, Tom?* Because I wanted to understand more, see more, examine the details of his existence. Perhaps like a zoologist who discovers a new, never before seen animal. He did slow to a near stop. Then his eyes, which I remember vividly, became impossibly big, deep and alive with creation. Not like the swirling images of the Universe we see in space movies, but the unimaginable power of creation. It was more of a boiling, surging and popping movement of loving energy. More alive than anything I've ever experienced or could imagine. Finally out of the swirling, spinning, exploding, entertaining and compelling mass of energy my image appeared which instantly formed the Jackalope back on the road jumping into the forest. This was precisely what I wanted to know. How did my Jackalope come into existence? I asked for him. I called him from the great sea of creation.

Everything exists within the Arc of Light. No matter where my interest took me, the choices available to me were beyond imagination, certainly beyond the concept of numbers. I was experiencing such delight in the flavors, tastes and sounds of one color of purple when I paused for a moment. I wondered to myself which color green would go with this purple. Purple, green and gold are particular favorites of mine. Without transition I was swimming in green. Examining an infinite sea of green streaming above, below, around and within me. Suddenly, the available greens displayed were reduced to the greens I liked best. This happened so organically it took a while to realize I had chosen these as favorites. Then each heavenly green color appeared in combination with my purple. Without further thought on my part variations of purple, green and gold appeared as if I were in some ultra-high tech design studio and I was choosing a color scheme for a project. It was like the Arc knew not only what I wanted, but also how I wanted to see all these colors displayed in various combinations. How I wanted the music of each separate color to combine with the others in a concert of overwhelming beauty and glory, uplifting and inspiring. At the same time, the Arc knew I wanted the flavors to blend into a taste sensation pleasing not only to my palate, but to others as well. As if I were serving all those I loved a sensational and satisfying feast in one heavenly color design. There were so many combinations of green and gold that fit beautifully with my purple I simply couldn't choose a favorite. Nor did I want to stop looking. It seemed like I could have spent eternity looking and sampling, but then a flash of realization jolted me from my search. I realized at that instant what it meant to have unlimited choices.

Infinite possibility.

Beyond Rich And Vibrant

You must know my experience was beyond our understanding of rich and vibrant. So rich and vibrant I could never adequately explain what I experienced if I continued every hour of every day for a millennium. All I can tell you is I wanted more. I wanted to feel more, see more, smell more, taste more, hear more, know more, do more, experience more. I had no longing, desire or even thought of returning. No regrets. None whatsoever. I was going home. I was happier than I'd ever known.

When I first looked up to The Arc of Light filling the darkness with brilliance, I knew it was coming especially for me. It was tailored to me. It knew everything about me. Everything I had ever done, said, thought, imagined or fantasized. Everything that can be known about me. Everything! Everything I had considered good and everything I considered bad. Everything I was proud I had done and everything I regretted. And then every nuance and extension connected to these experiences.

Time-space as we know it did not exist in the Arc. Consequently, I had no idea how long I was there. It seemed like weeks, months, maybe years, but it could have been less than a minute or a second in human time. How much time I spent in my death experience, and what happened when, is an absurd conversation. The road of time simply does not exist as we believe it does.

In The Presence

The Arc of Light was a venue for my audience. It was a backdrop, a moving, living stage for my audience with this amazingly beautiful, this awesome, incomparable Presence. A Presence whom I could not look upon directly because the brilliance of The Presence vastly exceeded that of the Arc of Light. Yet, they were one and the same. The Presence, however, was too intense, too powerful and too absolute. Description fails me. Words fail me. I was overpowered and humbled by the Presence.

You, too, may become overwhelmed in these pages as I attempt to convey my experience. Try to absorb the energy. That's what is important. Allow yourself to receive. What you feel as you read this chapter is a taste of the pure divine energy as I experienced it.

Remember: Before I could write this description I had to put myself back in that place and time. The information is important, but it's the energy that really raises your consciousness.

I would love to say the Presence was a celestial celebrity like Abraham, Krishna, Moses, The Great Spirit, Zoroaster, His Holiness Christ, Mohammed, The Divine Feminine, The Bab or Baha'u'llah. But I cannot. Those distinctions simply did not exist. The only awareness or understanding that came through was the Generous One. And that this distinction was inclusive, complete and perfect. All that existed was Unity. Separateness was nowhere to be found. Gender and character distinctions did not exist. Only The Light existed. The Light, The Presence of the Generous One, and I were all one. Regardless of what I had learned in Sunday School as a child, this was the Holy Trinity for me. The Light, The Presence and me. Joined in Divine Unity for eternity. I was with them, in them and through them. And They with me. We were all one together. We were One. There was no need for separation. No need for distinction. Only we existed in The Light. There was no Them or I. We were One. Much like your hands and feet are one with your body and your mind. I felt absolutely at peace, satisfied and complete. Infinitely empowered. I was joined with the Light and the Generous One, accepted and loved unconditionally for who I was and yet I remained humble as a suppliant in his Lord's court. I was never made to feel less or wanting or judged in any way. I was perfect in the Presence of Perfection. It was an amazing experience. I knew this Divine Audience I was awarded was the greatest blessing I could ever receive. That anyone could and would ever receive.

What's important is how I felt. I use felt for lack of a better word. Maybe disposition is better. By nature I have a curious, yet skeptical disposition. I am not a cynic. I am a cautious believer. Oh yes, I do often have six impossible beliefs before breakfast, but these are not necessarily my core beliefs. They are beliefs I try on for a while to see how they fit in my life. Beliefs in teleportation and our ability to heat and cool ourselves with our minds alone are today "impossible" beliefs. I'm still trying them on. They feel possible, especially since scientists have already teleported atoms over a distance equal to teleporting a 200-pound man across the Mississippi River above New Orleans, but I can't currently defend them for everyday use. Psychokinesis, the ability to move, affect or bend metal using only the power you can access with your mind is defensible. It is real. I have done it. I held two metal forks in my hand, told them to bend and they melted like butter. Using only quantum power I warmed and bent metal! So now the power of quantum energy is one of my core beliefs. It passed the test of possibility demanded by my cautious disposition.

When I entered into Divine Unity in the Court of The Presence of The Generous One I became completely open and willing to receive what was given me. I was like a dry sponge waiting to be immersed in the Ocean of Divine Healing. My caution evaporated in the brilliance of my environment. I was in The Presence of all truth. This I knew instantaneously. I was in the Presence of the essence of truth. A truth that was complete, pure and safe beyond any doubt or question. I had no need for analysis. I was glowing with joy. Free. Elevated. More elevated than you can possibly imagine. Elevated by my station which I had been granted among all that I was or ever could be. Not a title or a degree of attainment, but my station granted exclusively for me. I had absolutely no fear, no worry, no doubt, no need nor any desire to apologize or prove myself. The feeling of pure unconditional love that permeated my entire experience within The Arc of Light in the state of Divine Unity in The Presence of the Court of the Generous One empowered me in a way I would love to share with you. It made me feel like I could do anything. I knew that nothing was impossible; that all I had to do was imagine it and it would be so. I was within the realm of the power of infinity, within the Source of All Power and All Creation and yet, all that I experienced was only a taste of what was to come.

If we could hold that all-encompassing wonder of the Arc of Light in our hearts here in this world, for but a moment, we would open the door to a whole new earthly experience. We would never question infinite possibility again. Because what we consider as possibility here is simply a choice there. If you desired cold fission, it was yours. If you wanted a Jackalope, you got a Jackalope. If you wanted a world without cruelty, hatred and war, a simple choice would instantly open the door to lasting peace. The only instances in my life that even approached these feelings of joy, empowerment and absolute bliss were the moments of conception of each of my three children. For an instant I felt something divine and amazing passing through my wife and me. Yet, even that amazing experience comes in a far distant second to how I felt in the Presence of the Generous One. Now that I have written those words I realize that even the mention of a comparison is less than inadequate. It is feeble at best. It's like comparing a light bulb to a multitude of supernovas. My audience in the Presence of the Generous One in the Arc of Light was far beyond anything I can easily describe. Heavens, I'm still processing all this myself. Needless to say, encapsulating in words a meeting in the Presence of the Generous One must by its very nature remain a work in progress.

OK, take a breath and allow yourself time to process the energy of the Presence of the Generous One. These few pages are a lot to take in. The words and the subjects are of course important. The impact comes from the divine power of the energy of the encounter. I even get sleepy and the words seem to blur out as I read them. There's nothing like it in this world. Treat the rest of this chapter with patience and allow yourself the opportunity to embrace the energy. Take it slow and allow yourself time to process this taste of the divine energy of the Presence.

YouTube On Steroids

Most of my life I was told that when I died, I would be called to a reckoning and account for my sins, which I was assured were many. Standard boilerplate for growing up in the bible belt of the American Midwest. I had dreaded such a reckoning. I didn't believe the vivid claims of harsh punishments and torment promised for the unworthy, for those who strayed from "the strict and narrow path," for those who sinned. I never could accept such a harsh and angry God. Still, the threat of all that hellfire and damnation does have an effect over time. What if they were right? Would I be judged and found wanting? As many suggested to me personally, my next stop would be aboard a fast freight straight to hell.

Fortunately, no! From what I saw there was no fast freight filled with pitiful and tormented souls and no destination even remotely resembling hell.

I did face a reckoning, but much different than the horrors born in the dark ages of ignorance. My whole life experience played before me in a kind of living video, like YouTube on steroids. I re-experienced my entire life at the speed of light while at the same time watching myself as an observer from the outside. I experienced the thoughts and emotions I felt the first time, but I could also understand them objectively all at once. As my life played before me I was both relieved and excited. Much like receiving notes from the director after rehearsing a scene in a play or a movie. Every time a sequence came up I was worried about, perhaps a time when I had acted without the most noble of intentions, the most amazing thing happened. My living video would slow down and I would instantly understand each experience for what it really was. A learning opportunity. I would see the reason for the problem. How I handled it. What happened. What I learned. And how my life changed going forward. That's it.

I never felt one single bit of judgment or condemnation. Ever!!!

Without narration my life passed before my consciousness. The knowledge I gleaned was more by assimilation than instruction. I would view a sequence and come to understand the message. Truly a story told in pictures. The living video began with two strangers meeting seemingly by chance in a café in a small town north of Omaha. My birth mother and father were drawn together powerfully, inescapably against all odds. She was a lonely Dutch Protestant farmwoman who'd lost her husband in the war. He was a lonely Irish Catholic salesman from Boston. At that time and in that place there was no gulf greater than existed between Catholic and Protestant. I was conceived in the heat and passion of forbidden love. A love that was limited from the start.

I was the fruit of that love. As an adoptee I had always been troubled – no, more than that – I have always been tormented by my abandonment. I always thought my father left me before the sheets were changed. Cold, uncaring and heartless. No loyalty. No integrity. An inherently selfish person I swore I'd never emulate and didn't. Or at least I didn't think I did. Then my mother put me up for adoption almost immediately. How could she do that?! Was she as heartless? Or was she simply desperate? Was he just out for a good time without any concern for my mother or me? Leaving us alone to face the social embarrassment and humiliation of the unmarried pregnancy? Was she too embarrassed by me, the fruit of her illicit affair? Is that why she had to turn her back on me and abandoned me to my own resources? Did she lack the courage to stand and face the world with a bastard son? Was I too ugly, tainted with her sin? This pain had gone a long way to forge my life, my personality.

Nothing was farther from the truth. In the span of nanoseconds I saw and knew the truth that I had misunderstood all my whole life. They were very much in love, but she was Protestant and alone. He was Catholic with a loveless marriage in Boston. They did what they had to do. He went back east and she never told him about me. Then she gave me up because my path led where she couldn't go. I felt their pain and I saw the sacrifice they both made. They couldn't fight the mores of their time. Their love had been beautiful and brief with one winning outcome – me.

I needed to grow up in the safety and protection of farm conservative Nebraska. My work, my path was set before my conception. The adopting parents who chose me as I chose them showered me with love and gave me the room I needed to grow and question. They gave me the opportunity to stay open to possibility. I can't really explain everything I knew in the instant

I experienced that video, but I can say this is where my healing began. In a moment of insight so many things became clear.

I saw the alternative choices of parents that might have occurred and the consequences of those choices. But I couldn't follow them very far; they faded quickly. Still, I realized the choice I had made was to my lasting benefit. Yes, I chose those birth parents and the consequences that followed. It's amazing how much choice you have even before, during and after your conception.

All this was so quick. So positive. So completely satisfying to my interest and enlightenment. I understood the importance and design of my life. I had always been burdened by a wounded self-image as the creature of a mistake, the result of deception and folly, a foundling lucky to have anything. I saw how this misunderstanding of reality hindered my growth in some ways and strengthened me in other ways.

Limited Understanding

We all misunderstand much of our life's experience; that's part of our challenge in the earthly experience. This is why the gift I bring is so incredibly important to you. It will help you gain a better perspective, a softer, more loving understanding of the events of your life's journey.

As my living video moved forward, I saw my first love when I was eighteen, obviously a learning experience. I was surprised then when the video slowed for my review until I realized I had never really released the pain of my rejection. Her parents felt threatened by me. They felt we weren't right for each other. They were right. I was shown that this experience was necessary for me to be ready when the real love of my life came along. Without the intensity of that relationship and my subsequent loss and pain, I would not have acted as quickly in asking Diane to marry me. We always joked about the fact that I proposed only six weeks after we met. The video showed me why I did act so quickly. Diane was absolutely my divine compliment. She already had a contract to teach school in California. She was strong and eager to move forward with her life. If I had hesitated I may have lost her for many years. Severely altering my path and hers. We would have reconnected many years later because we were meant to help each other in this experience, but it wouldn't have been the same. Somehow our union made her life and mine cleaner, purer in its direction. I was so full of creative energy, headstrong, determined to do things my way while distrusting authority of any kind. I could easily have spent years trudging among the tall grasses and lost in the dark, dense woods along the fairway of my life's path. Diane was given to me in part to keep me safe from myself while I learned what I needed to learn to do my work. The work I'm doing now.

Why I was given to her still only God knows.

Now I need to make it abundantly clear that what I saw, what I experienced was for my benefit, my consciousness. I have absolutely no idea what would apply to your life. We are all individuals. Our paths are different. Maybe there's one partner for you, maybe two or three. I don't know. I do know life is fluid. It is not rigid. Nothing is cut and dried. Nothing is simple. There are choices and consequences to learn from. My living video was giving me feedback on my choices and what I learned. I don't know where Diane's path might have taken her or where yours might take you.

I examined many more incidents in my life. Including more would serve no purpose other than to pique your curiosity about me and that is not why I wrote this book. I have included two scenes so that you might understand one simple fact. Nothing about your life is as cut and dried as you might think. You are important and the things that happen to you are important to you. Important to who you are. Important because ... well, you do know who you are, right? You remember.

In these important, lasting and precious moments I saw how my actions affected the lives of others. I realized that I, too, was merely one of their life experiences. The harm I had imagined I caused others was for them a learning opportunity. Oh, what a difference love makes. I was expecting hellfire and damnation, but instead got discernment, insight, perception and the wisdom of understanding my own personal experiences in the perspective of becoming a more powerful, elevated being.

Experiences I had considered damning, for decades, lost all power to elicit guilt and fear. I was heartened that what I'd come to believe over the years was essentially true. You and I are not here in this world to please an angry God. We are here to grow and learn. We are here to advance and gain a more expansive and more far-reaching and elevated consciousness. To learn divine attributes, which allow us to better align with and grow closer to the Source of All-Creation. We are here to become a more complete and transcendent being.

Now, I must admit that processing and releasing those damning experiences back here in this temporal matrix took some work. I had to face my own past and make amends for the misdeeds I believed I created. Only then could I release the past and fully appreciate the lesson I had been given. I told you I was headstrong. I tell myself that's my Dutch side, no doubt about it. Of course, it is the veil of separateness that negatively and needlessly influences us all.

As my living video came to an end I eagerly awaited giving my decision. No one in his or her right mind would give up all this beauty and peace for the world I left behind. Of course, I would go on. Of course, I would choose death. Death was the only life worth living.

As another living video started, I saw myself lying in the hospital room prodding Penelope to take my picture shortly before having the stroke that brought me here. The thought that had raced through my mind as my life was being squeezed from my body. The thought I'd never expressed. My last earthly thought and desire burst into my thoughts.

Oh no! I wanted to say goodbye to Diane.

Instantly, to an ear splitting sound similar to fingernails scraping across a blackboard, I was pulled back from paradise. Pulled back from the rich, vivid and serene beauty of my heavenly interlude to the noise, chaos, frustration, tests and difficulties of my earthly experience. Back from unconditional love, joy and divine peace. Back to the land of hate and violence, of separation and differences. Back to the land of pain and suffering.

It took longer to adjust to earth than it had to heaven. It seemed like hours as I became aware of my body again, the paralyzed body I'd left behind. I became aware of the syncopation of the monitors, of the noisy chatter of the doctors and nurses as they congratulated themselves while filing out of the Emergency Room where I'd taken my last breath. I was dazed and confused. Not sure what happened or why I was here. Everything seemed so flat and limited and murky.

They left the electrical harness glued to my chest. The nurses were gone, and my kids were once again coming into my room when the doctor in charge looked at me and with the great satisfaction of having pulled someone from the clutches of the Grim Reaper and defeated Dreaded Death itself, said,

"We thought we lost you there for a minute."

CHAPTER 11

Some Assembly Required

The gift I promised to bring back for you. The unique and wonderful gift that can elevate and empower your life. The gift of Miracle Healing consecrated in the Presence of the Generous One requires more than reading, understanding and a willingness to accept. Oh, it requires all that, but it requires a little bit more.

Some assembly is required.

This gift will not activate for you if you keep it strictly an intellectual exercise. This world is all about what you do, not about what you think. The power of your mind is beyond measure, but thinking alone will never produce the results you desire until you take action. It is acting that generates the good you seek. This is what many refer to as manifesting your good. You can hold a positive attitude, you can visualize what you desire, you can write down your desires all you want, but unless you take action those desires cannot manifest themselves in your life. If you ask for a new car, for example, it will not magically appear in your driveway. You must do something. You must actively look for your car or talk about your car or act as a friend and help others or enter a raffle. You must do something. It is your action that becomes the catalyst for creation.

As with all things in this world receiving the myriad bounties your gift holds requires your action. You cannot simply read and receive. This book is not a distraction from your daily grind. It is not a fun fantasy about what might be possible someday. It is not only an interesting story about one person's experience. It is first and foremost an amazing gift you asked to receive. Unless you take action that gift cannot reach you. The laws of cause and effect are real and immutable. Besides the actions you must take are very simple and quite enjoyable. They are more like treating yourself to a moment of enlightenment and bliss than going to work.

First, take some time to process what you just read. Examine your own feelings. This is the road to personal enlightenment. Did my account of my death experience open the doors to any questions you may have buried deep in your consciousness? Did you experience any conflicts with your own beliefs? Did anything here make you feel anxious, angry, uneasy, conflicted or confused? Did my account of my death experience answer any questions you may have had? Did it give you comfort, solace, guidance, direction or confirmation? Spend some time with yourself working through your feelings. Do you accept what you've read as true and good? Do you reject all or some? This is the key to open the door of a greater understanding and awareness of who you are and why you are here.

You are building a better life. Know what you are working with so you can assemble the parts carefully.

I know reading my own account of my experience was both enlightening and empowering for me. When I started writing this book I had no idea what was waiting for me. Even when I finished what I thought was the final draft. I gained the satisfaction of completing what turned out to be a rough draft, but it was only after I processed the work and examined my personal feelings that my consciousness grew perceptibly. Yes, I gained a lot from the experience itself, but it was elementary compared to what I gained after I processed the information and remembered what I needed to bring my efforts to a conclusion. Processing is a major component to your growth and expansion.

Remember this information is for you as much as it is for me. Let it work in your heart and your mind. Life is too short to pass up such a rare and priceless gift as this one.

Secondly, you must take an active participation in your gift. This gift is like that new car you desired above. It is beautiful. It is exactly the car for you. It has the potential for taking you anywhere you want to go, meetings, parties, great adventures. None of which can happen until you start the engine and put it in gear. You must take action. The same is true of the gift I have brought back for you. Until you take action and send Tom a healing message back in the early morning hours of March 29, 2009 in the Presence of the Generous One your amazing gift must forever remain merely potential. A good idea gone to waste. A could have been. A lost opportunity for greatness.

You must actually open your mouth and send your healing message.

So do it already!

Let's try it just for fun.

Participate in your own healing. You'll love it. We'll make it very, very simple.

Open your mouth and say these three words.

Heal. Heal. Heal.

Out loud, please. Quietly if you have to, but vocalize them.

These are good words; nobody will be offended. Say them out loud. Engage your personal strength.

Heal. Heal. Heal.

One more time, please. I cannot tell you how important this is for all of us.

This time put some real feeling into your effort.

Say: Heal. Heal. Heal.

Come on. Again. This time say it like you mean it. You're healing someone, for goodness sake.

With gusto!

Heal! Heal! Heal!

Great.

Now, close you eyes and think of Tom needing your help, this very instant. He needs your healing message right now.

Say: Heal! Heal! Heal!

Picture your healing message zooming across time and space to join that brilliant rainbow of Miracle Healing besieging Tom at this very moment.

Thank you. Thank you. Thank you.

Congratulations.

You did it.

You sent your first Miracle Healing.

As you will soon see, your timing couldn't be better.

CHAPTER 12
Inherit The Earth

After the doctors and nurses left the Emergency Room, everything grew foggy. It seemed like one of those thick coastal fogs had hit Saddleback Memorial. As they rolled me out of that little room, the fog rolled in, whiting out first my family, then everything beyond my immediate vision, then the orderly pushing my bed, then nothing. I don't remember anything else. I think it was just too much for my injured brain to handle. I was back on earth. Paradise had slipped away and I was back here, like it or not. When the hard reality of my terribly damaged condition started to sink in I simply checked out, hoping and praying I'd wake up and this living nightmare would vanish with the morning light.

No such luck.

My drooling, gurgling, half-dead body and what was left of my badly injured brain were headed to ICU, where they would attach more wires, tubes and well-meaning implements of torture designed to keep me breathing and alive. I no longer had control of my own life. I was at their mercy.

There was no hell waiting after death. Why should there be? We have Earth. And apparently I had chosen it.

My Romantic New Beginning Wasn't

ICU was very large compared to my Emergency Room cubicle. ICU was about 25'X25' and very, very sterile. It had a private bathroom off to my right. I never saw the inside, but it seemed large also. I remember thinking my room would make a good master bedroom and wondering why they wasted all this space on one person. Strange thought for someone having trouble coming to grips with reality. Sharing the room were a number of very impressive pieces of medical equipment, which they rolled up to my bed as they needed them. There weren't chairs for people visiting. I guess visiting was restricted. The most impressive feature of the room was the wall to my left. It was all glass and it faced a large curved workstation for the doctors and nurses. I know it should have been comforting to know my keepers could keep an eye on me 24/7, but it didn't. I felt like a caged animal in some ancient episode of *Twilight Zone*. I was being held against my wishes.

The colors in ICU were muted, gray upon more gray. I had just come from an explosion of color and there was definitely no gray involved. In fact, I don't remember seeing gray at all. A place of healing should overflow with bright, cheerful colors to engage the mind and encourage its participation. It is, after all, our minds that allow the healing to take place, and it is our bodies that do the work. Colors that celebrate life invigorate and inspire the mind. Gray, muted or lifeless colors, weak tints that can't seem to decide what they are or what they are meant to accomplish discourage and invite the mind to give up and shun the hard work ahead. The sounds were also counter to healing. The dominant sounds were of the lower order, noises made by machines locked in steel, glass and plastic. These were the uncaring, uninspired, monotonous sounds exhibiting the characteristics of lifelessness, hopelessness and despair. Where was the music of a new dawn breaking over the mountaintops? Or sounds of the sea sculpting the shoreline? Or the laughter of children, the chirp of crickets, the flutter of wings or the buzzing of bees? These sounds encourage life and healing. The odors that welcomed me back were the scent of antiseptic and chemicals covering biological distress. Where were the roses, the first cutting of freshly mown alfalfa or sea air in the early morning as the sun rises across the beach? I wanted to escape, get away, run, but I could barely move my head to take in a few pieces of crushed ice to quench my thirst.

My return was a rude awaking. I had always felt like I was living a miracle life. I felt like I was protected from real pain. Hardship, yes. Difficulties, sure. Physical debilitation, no. How can you live a productive life when you are so terribly weakened and impaired? I had been following my calling. I was working for the Cause of God. Telling folks how they could get rich using practical applications of Universal Laws. How they could live a rich abundant life without losing their integrity, time or family. How they could lift themselves to a higher level of consciousness. Of course, I was protected.

I had to be protected.

Boy, was I mistaken. I definitely had not gotten a pass on the physical hardship thing. The question that permeated my thoughts was, "What have I done wrong?"

The same question I had always counseled my students to reject. I felt that all my pain and suffering was surely some kind of punishment. It had to be! I certainly wouldn't ask for this.

Even experiencing an afterlife void of punishment of any kind wouldn't calm my mind. I was processing.

I cannot imagine what it is like for the men and women wounded mentally, emotionally or physically in battle to process their experiences. Some don't process them and relive their horror every day for years. My heart goes out to them. They are stronger than I am. I do know that what they have gone through is not their fault and they have done absolutely nothing wrong. I knew a man in Hobbs, New Mexico, who couldn't get past his experience in Viet Nam. He took his own life. I have known several good people and one good friend who opened heaven's gate before their work here was finished. I certainly do not encourage this option, but neither can I judge them. Most of the time that option is not on the table. Loss of hope can put that option back on the table.

After that sixth stroke, orderlies had once again rolled me down that long hall with all its twists and turns to the CAT Scan room. Eventually, they took me back to ICU, where doctors pronounced me paralyzed for life and useless beyond hope. Destined for twenty years of bed rest.

By some miracle I did manage to connect with Diane that night. I woke and she stood next to me. I'd heard the doctor's prognosis of my condition and prospects of healing which were bleak. I don't know how I heard. I'm positive they hadn't told me. I was treated more like a mushroom than a partner in my own healing. I remember crying as Diane held me. Crying my heart out. Between sobs I told her I was so sorry for doing this to her. That there were so many things I needed to say. That it might have been better if I had died. I was, however, mostly making gurgling noises, so she didn't hear it. She just held me and told me, "Everything will be all right." She said it over and over again. I tried to explain that all our hopes and dreams were gone. *Everything will be all right.* I wanted her to know that I was now only a burden. That I was sorry, so very sorry for everything. *Everything will be all right.* I begged her forgiveness because I couldn't hold her, but my words were little more than wet noise. *Everything will be all right.* Then, I told her I came back to tell her goodbye. Apparently, all she heard was goodbye because she squeezed me harder and told me, "Don't say that, Tom. We will beat this. We've come through so much already. You will get better. I promise. You will get better."

I remember thinking, "I don't think so, my love, not this time. Not this time." That thick fog drifted back into the room and slowly Diane dissolved into the mind numbing grey of nothingness.

That first night my living nightmare continued. I was in and out of awareness all night long. I mostly remember those horrid plastic cuffs they put around my legs. Every ten minutes or so they would fill with air and squeeze my legs for another ten minutes. This was intended to prevent blood clots. As soon as the leg squeezers stopped I would drift into what served as sleep. Half awake, half-asleep, it was like my essence was outside my body the whole time trying to return to my physical presence, but I needed sleep for that to happen and sleep was nearly impossible in ICU. The automated blood pressure cuff was also fun. It would wake me again by tightly squeezing my arm. First one device then the other denied my escape into the oblivion of sleep. I don't have any idea exactly what the time schedules of those devices were. I only remember that they were terribly annoying. I wanted to sleep desperately. They told me later that you heal only when you sleep. I could have used a little healing right then, but those wretched leg squeezers and cuff helped make for a very tortured night.

Life In The Hospital Isn't

In the yellow-green glow of the monitors, the empty sterile and deathly cold expanse of the ICU room, I faced my hell. Although at the time I had no idea where I was. It felt like a place of punishment and enduring pain. That room seemed big like a storage vault. Was I dead in a morgue somewhere? Was I cursed to a nether world of living horror? Had I missed my chance to go on? Was I alive? If so, where?

It takes longer to adjust to earth than heaven.

I drifted in and out of consciousness. I would alternately re-experience my Interview in the Presence of the Generous One, and then I would quickly cut to the harsh reality of my condition. Or back to my living YouTube video, replaying the segments for which I had feared retribution and damnation. For a while I was back in Hobbs, New Mexico, lying in the middle of my carpet warehouse on somebody's used carpet surrounded by the people I had seen in my Living Video, the ones I felt I'd wronged. They didn't say anything. They just stood there and looked down at me. I wanted to tell them I did my best, but I couldn't. I still felt that caustic shame and guilt I always had. Like I said it took a lot of work to process the clearing I had experienced. Nothing made sense. I couldn't focus. I couldn't distinguish one reality from another as I apparently drifted among many.

In the end I saw no hope. No chance to live a full and productive life. No chance to play with my grandkids, party with friends and family or take my wife out to dinner and dancing. Then the plague of regret started. I hadn't taken her out to dinner and dancing enough when I could have. All I could think of was loss and despair. I was filled with scarcity consciousness. I was convinced my life was over. I had become nothing more than a liability. I wanted out. Why spend another night in this world of horror? I wanted to leave this cruel, painful and utterly irrational existence we call life. I wanted to go home, back to the peace and serenity of The Arc of Light, back to the Court of The Presence of the Generous One and say, "Yes, I'm ready. Take me home."

I asked to die.

CHAPTER 13

The Message

In the next life, you don't have the pressures you do here. There is no need to make money, pay bills or save for old age. No need to work hard, take care of your body or help others who are less fortunate than you. No need to go to school, find your passion or overcome tests and difficulties. No need to discover anything. Create anything. Build anything. No need to gain anything or lose anything. There's no need to love, be loved or raise children. No need to feel emotions of any kind. And there's definitely no need to work on your golf swing or have your nails done because you won't have any arms, legs or fingers. Nope, in the next life you are not burdened by any of that in the slightest. These are all uniquely human experiences. Experiences that lead you to make choices. Choices made possible only because free will is inherent to the matrix of our earthly experience. Choices that shape your life and give you a unique and fleeting opportunity to grow and learn. Choices, which ultimately extend your awareness and expand your consciousness.

Because as you grow, as your choices and their subsequent consequences lead you to a more elevated human experience, your eternal essence becomes more aligned with the energy of the Ultimate Power of all Creation. This is the essence of healing. This is how you know who you are.

You Chose

Cherish the life you are given. You came here at this experiential, phenomenal point in our growth as a culture to strengthen and expand your unique essence. You were given talents and abilities consistent with the work that needs to be done now. Right now. You came here to face challenges, make choices, live with the consequences and in so doing raise your consciousness, and in so doing the consciousness of the whole of humanity. This is the process by which you come to know who you are. And knowing who you are is the lynchpin to attracting your Miracle Healing.

To fully understand who you are you must know one very important fact:

You chose to come here.

Yes, you chose to come here at the exact moment, place and parentage of your birth to face the challenges and benefits for growth only available at that precise moment of our time-space matrix. No mistakes, accidents nor anything even remotely random are involved. You chose to come here and now. This is your challenge. This is your time. This is your opportunity. You won't get this opportunity in the next life. There are no choices in the next life. No challenges. No victories. No defeats. No reflections. No revelations. No celebrations. There are no consequences, no growing, no learning, at least, not as we know it in this earthly experience. I cannot testify to the possibility you will go on to another world once you pass through the Arc of Light. That information was not made available to me. Of course, why wouldn't there be other worlds? We are dealing with infinity. All I'm saying is take advantage of the uniquely precious gifts of this temporal, material matrix while you can. What fool leaves a diamond mine with their pockets full of coal?

You came here so your essence could mature. So you could become more aligned with the energy of All-Creation. This transformational playground, this amazing and miraculous venue for growth and development we call earth is a bounty given to us by the Generous One as an aid for our advancement. It is here to provide you with the opportunity to try, fail and succeed, so you can experience and grow from the consequences of your choices.

Talisman for Change

Remember: You Are The One! You are the talisman that opens the door to fulfilling centuries of prophecy. You – not your children or their children – you and I are the groundbreakers who must prepare for the building of a self-perpetuating, ever abundant paradise on earth. It is up to you and me to heal ourselves, our kind and eventually our planet from thousands of years of growing pains. The best part is, what's required of you is not difficult.

You are not an accident.

You are eternal. You hold within you the power to cause anything to happen. You are supported always, regardless of what you may feel, think or believe. You are never alone. Never. In your darkest hour of need ask for help and it is given, instantly. You can have absolutely anything you want to have, including Jackalopes. If you can imagine it, you can have it. The only limits placed upon your desires are those you impose on yourself. You are an amazingly powerful being with an equally amazing sphere of influence. You are Rich Beyond Your Wildest Dreams! So why not act like it? Since you can have anything you desire, why not behave as a generous, loving, responsible adult who is using your precious few hours here in this glorious time-space matrix as an opportunity to elevate your life? Why not elevate the lives of your fellow human beings? Why not elevate your brothers and sisters everywhere, children and grandchildren and all those who will come after you. Regardless of their differences. Regardless of their opinions. Regardless of the good or the bad we believe they generate or inspire. *You are not an accident; neither are they.* Why not choose the high road? When you can already have anything you want? Anything! Why not choose to elevate all that you can see, touch, feel, hear, smell and taste? And all that you cannot see, touch, feel, hear, smell and taste? Love each and every member of your human family. We need everybody. United we are even more powerful. Elevate and hold precious all that is, regardless, of your personal beliefs, preferences or choices. Because those ugly, hateful disgusting people, ideas and things you see all around you are nothing more than reflections in a mirror.

Admit to yourself exactly how powerful and amazingly rich you truly are, as frightening as that may seem.

While writing this book I faced many seemingly dire circumstances. I'm writing this for all of us, remember. I must feel these things deep in my essence, so I've been blessed with an abundance of tests and difficulties. These tests and difficulties are divine gifts, all given to me for my growth. Of course, that doesn't make them sting any less.

In desperation one day I asked God – well, more like shouted, "What am I doing wrong? I have written down my requests. I have surrendered to your will. Yet, I am plagued with unbearable difficulties. I never stop working to alter my situation, but nothing changes. What can I do? Just tell me Lord and I will do it! Tell me, what should I do?"

The answer came quickly. I am one of those lucky people who hear voices. I don't know who They are exactly, guides or angels. But they really do cut to the chase.

They answered:

"You [humans] don't get it. We [Guides/Angels] don't have free will. We wait for your direction. We can only step in and help if we are asked. If you try to do it yourself, we cannot interfere.

That is what letting go is. That is what surrender is.

When you ask for help and allow help, anything can happen. Anything. We can do anything. We can make anything happen.

It is not up to you to know how to make anything happen. It is up to you to know how to ask and let go. Then, and only then, can we go to work."

Obviously, I had not let go. I had not surrendered. Sometimes we only let go when everything seems hopeless. When we have tried and failed and tried some more, and are in a place of desperation. Only when we have reached the end of our rope with nowhere to go are we in a place where we can say, "I surrender " and honestly mean it. Sometimes, it's only out of desperation that we learn the true meaning of detachment.

This is where the planet and we are right now. In a place of desperation. You don't want to see that, of course, but it's true. We are at a crossroads. We are all in a place of desperation, you, and me – everybody. Our opportunities for living in infinite abundance are dwindling in direct proportion to the number of animal and plant species lost to extinction every year. Earth, our delightful, living, breathing transformational playground for growth, is in need of our making better choices. We have taken paradise and leveled it for parking lots, quick profits and temporal power.

It was not a pretty video I was shown when I ascended the second time. Horrors I prefer not to discuss. Horrors we have the power to prevent, if we simply do what we came here to do.

Seek An Elevated Life

In my pain and anguish that first night in ICU, I had asked to die. I didn't ask that my pain go away. I didn't ask for help or guidance. No, in a moment of incredible lack of wisdom I asked to die. I asked to cash in my much sought after membership to the human experience. I asked to be released from the opportunity to grow and learn to play in earth's transformational playground. When the going got rough I didn't ask for more stuff. I gave up hope. I forgot why I was here. I was ready to give up my chance to expand my consciousness, to elevate my station and grow closer to the Power and Beauty of the Glorious One, all for the sake of an easy way out of my current discomfort. What's 20 years of bed rest compared to an eternity without physical experiences of any kind, without growth of any kind? Do not seek death. Seek life. Seek an elevated life.

Instead, I sought death and death I received. Again.

The overture for my second death experience was much less dramatic than the first. In fact, I left my body before I felt or heard a thing. I missed all the beeping, buzzing, rushing and talking. I left in my uneasy sleep. I don't remember leaving my body, just having left my body. I guess you don't need as much preparation for a willing soul. My destination was not a mystery. I was well prepared for where I was going. Again, my pains and fears evaporated, instantly. I floated above the ICU briefly in that same delicious, quiet blackness as before. I watched as the staff of nurses and doctors rushed to my body's rescue. God bless them for their caring effort and for keeping my body alive while I made my choice.

Quickly, my attention shifted to the Arc of Light. I don't remember the same images I had the first time. I don't remember the long tunnel descending from above. I don't remember the fantastic sounds, the intriguing flavors, the empowering aromas, the intoxicating colors. I'm sure that vivid texture of senses I witnessed the first time was still there. It's just that was not the compelling memory I brought back with me. Something far more dominating was impressed on my essence.

I turned up and I was in the Arc. That's all I remember. It seemed my awareness of the Arc of Light and my intention of returning was all that was necessary for admittance. I welcomed the warm and loving embrace of the Arc and merged easily with Its awesome beauty and majesty. Once again, Supreme Intelligence surrounded and infused my eternal being. I was eager to go on. I had decided. My mind was made up. I had said goodbye to my wife. I was no longer encumbered.

I was concerned, however, with her future welfare. How would she get along without me? Would she suffer? Would she miss me? I'd always been the moneymaker. Would she find someone else? How would the kids do? Would they miss me? Would Alex find his place in the culture he both ridiculed and loved? Would he be happy? Would he find lasting love? Would he get the opportunity to raise a child and be the father he always hoped he would be? Would his maturation and success be as difficult and painful as mine had been? Would Heather find her place in the world? Would she find a permanent, abiding love? Would my passing hurt her more than the others? She'd been so fragile in the Emergency Room. Would she find the strength to accept and love herself? Would Penelope gain the self-confidence to continue to use her amazing talents without me breaking down the doors? Would they all accept their own incredible value and importance? Would they brighten the world as they have brightened my life?

I wondered about Lucy, my granddaughter. What would become of her? Would she grow up to be strong and have kids of her own? What would she give to the world? Would she remember me? My grandson, Finn, was not yet born. What would he look like? What would his talents and nature be? Would the others tell him about me? Would he care? Would anyone care? Would I simply be forgotten after the grieving process was over? Would I have given them anything of lasting importance?

Follow The Yellow Brick Road

My interest was initially focused on my family's future. That was the first Living Video I was shown. As with my first death experience I could both observe and enter these Living Videos as an unseen participant, simultaneously. I saw my funeral. More people came than I thought possible. I was really stunned and pleased. My focus, however, was on Diane and the kids. I saw them grieve. I watched each of my children grow into their prime. I watched them find success, happiness and lasting love. I saw my grandkids grow and flourish. Oh, they all had their share of tests and difficulties, but from my vantage point nothing seemed out of kilter. I'm not sure I can explain this properly, but I'll try. I saw them each face obstacles along their path, which, of course, is expected. What was strange was that they did seem to be following a pre-designed path. I know I say that all the time, "Oh, God open Thou the door, provide the means, make safe the path and guide my way." From the Living Video it seemed like each individual was indeed traveling a set course or path. They made various choices along the way. They moved and changed direction as they made these choices, but they never seemed to stray beyond certain invisible parameters. Like they were on a pre-defined journey, which encompassed a wide degree of variables, yet led in a given direction. The journey was dictated by the individual's choices, and when these choices took the individual off course the consequences were intended to guide him back on his general course. There was sort of a fuzzy logic involved. I could tell it was a designated path, but I cannot explain how I knew that. It just was.

Each individual seemed to grow stronger as they negotiated their path, which makes sense. As they grew stronger they also grew bigger and brighter. I mean physically more imposing and visually more striking. They seemed to radiate this growth and brilliant stature. It was remarkable to watch. Yet, even more remarkable was the greening and enhancement of their path as the individuals grew stronger, bigger. Their surroundings seemed to reflect their personal growth.

No, it was more than merely reflecting the individual's condition. Their environment seemed to remake itself better and bolder with each step. The obstacles laid in their paths seemed to materialize as they approached a given spot. It was as though they had been guided to that area on their path where they would face a pre-determined obstacle. Like they were now prepared by their experiences to handle the obstacle that had been pre-chosen by them for them to face. What's more, the obstacles seemed to lack substance. My best simile is that they were like CGI Tigers, generated by some Divine computer program. They had shape and form, but they simply lacked substance. Oh, many held a threat that was quite real, but nothing the individual could not handle. Much like the problems Dorothy encountered on her path to find the Wizard of Oz. The threats were a stimulus that helped Dorothy and her friends understand they already held the solution within them to overcome the challenges they faced. It was like each member of my family was a player in a high-end video game of Follow the Yellow Brick Road tailored exclusively for him or her. It was both eerie and confirming. Of course, I didn't see them complete their journeys. I don't know how much they grew. How radiant they became. Or if they lost ground on their journey and reverted to a lesser radiance. The Living Videos ended too quickly.

In retrospect, I wondered, if I had turned my attention and interest to myself, would I have seen my stroke and witnessed the extent and degree of my miracle recovery and my success in fulfilling my mission? Of course, I didn't know I had a mission at that point. I was still planning to leave this mortal coil behind and seek the multiple dimensions of green in the pastures above.

Maybe I cared more about my family than myself. It's a moot point. I didn't ask about me.

I saw Diane grieve. Then she went on with her life. I don't think I can talk about her. It hurts too much to know how much I would miss her. Of course, that is a human emotion I am applying to an otherworldly experience. I intended to follow her through the rest of her life, but the video also ended abruptly. This time I knew I was not allowed to see any more details because I had not made my final decision. So, the events that shaped the rest of her life could not have happened. And because the physical world was in a time of great change, so also, was the future in tremendous flux. Honestly, some of what I experienced in those few moments was clarifying and enlightening. Other parts are mystifying and created more questions than answers. I wondered about that. If I was in a place to know all there was to know, why then could I not know some things?

Writing Your Future

That's when I was given the next video. It started strangely enough with a scene in a movie theater. I had taken my family to *Back to the Future III* in Huntington Beach in the early '90s. The movie was almost over. Christopher Lloyd was delivering a line all the kids considered super sappy, but one that impacted me more than I apparently knew. He said, "Your future hasn't been written yet. No one's has. Your future is whatever you make it. So make it a good one." Immediately, the video cut to a forest fire. A huge storm of forest fires engulfing everything in their path as they sweep across the United States, Brazil, the Congo, Southern

Asia and Northern Russia and most of Eastern Europe. I saw earthquakes in San Francisco, Mexico City, Denver, Caracas, Tokyo, Singapore, Santiago and across the Pacific Rim. I saw volcanoes spewing hot lava and people running. I saw islands exploding, cities burning, billions of hectares of dirt and ash covering the noonday sky. I saw ice storms in London, Moscow, Paris and New York City. Incredibly powerful super oceanic storms devastating coastlines around the globe. Epic flooding. Fighting in the street. Frightened people running and fighting everywhere. Chaos, death and horror reigned. As I watched my overwhelming emotion was one of terrible sadness. The effect of a planet trying to heal itself. I saw more death and horror than any Hollywood disaster movie could ever believably depict. And through it all I kept hearing that movie line from so long ago. *"Your future hasn't been written yet. No one's has. Your future is whatever you make it. So make it a good one."*

I didn't want to talk about that video because no one really believes doomsday prophesies. We discount these images as pure histrionics. We know all too well that bad things can and do happen to good people and we prefer to banish these images from our minds for fear that we attract that reality into our own lives. As entertainment disasters movies can be fun as long as the hero survives, leaving someone else to clean up the mess, of course. I had resolved to avoid telling this video, but They wouldn't let that happen. Because you absolutely must recognize the fact that our current behavior as individuals and as a culture is leading us along a path which if unaltered, will lead to one inevitable, awful destination.

They want me to make it abundantly clear, if I haven't already, that none of this horrific possibility need ever happen. *"Your future hasn't been written yet. No one's has. Your future is whatever you make it. So make it a good one."*

I had asked for death so I could slip painlessly into eternity. I had wanted to spend my forever relishing the colors, the aromas, the tastes and beauty of all I could explore. I intended to go to a better place where I would leave annoying human problems behind. I saw paradise as a kind of gated, spiritual, retirement community. Collect my good works pension and bask in the glory forever after. I came to realize that was another pipe dream. *You are not an accident.* The problems wouldn't go away because you leave. They wouldn't solve themselves. My leaving meant that someone else would be required to do my job as well as their own. Besides, part of me was still living on earth in the DNA of my children and grandchildren. So, I wouldn't be avoiding the problem at all. I was just wasting my opportunity to do something worthwhile and meaningful. I was spending my progeny's future needlessly in a moment of selfishness. What's more, I would have denied myself the healing I came into the earth experience to enjoy.

What Could I Do?

I am merely a single individual in a sea of billions. I came here at this moment in our evolution with certain talents and abilities and I was leaving before my part was complete, before my job was finished. *You are not an accident.* I was not meeting my responsibility to my family, my friends and my kind. Most importantly, I was cutting myself short. I was denying myself the opportunity to transform into the spiritual being I had come here to become. The being that I was meant to be. The being that I thought I was before the stroke. I was leaving my path before I got to my ultimate destination. I was giving up. I was not bringing my actions to a conclusion. That weighed on me not as guilt, but as the gut wrenching sadness of missed opportunity and neglected responsibility.

But what could I do?

I was only one man, a severely disabled man at that. I couldn't talk, write, sit up, walk, feed or dress myself. What kind of change could I generate? Certainly not enough to change the world; that was simply ludicrous. One man cannot change the world. That's a fairy tale meant for a super hero stories. OK, Manifestations of God like Moses, the Friend of God; His Holiness Christ, the Son of God; Mohammed, the Prophet of God and Baha'u'llah, the Glory of God, brought vast, sweeping worldwide change. I get that, but I was nothing close to them. I was a man filled with imperfections, defects of character, and personal ambitions, which do not put me anywhere near Their station. I didn't have the serenity and Divine Wisdom of Buddha nor of Krishna nor the many spiritual giants that have empowered and guided our civilization. It was patently absurd. I knew I was making the right decision. There was nothing else I could do. I had to go on. I had to leave fixing the world to somebody richer, smarter, stronger, better established, better connected. Maybe somebody in the next generation would handle this better than I can. I was leaving.

I had lost track of the amazing sensual displays, the vast repositories of knowledge waiting only for my interest to explore. I forgot everything surrounding me in this glorious, unending wealth of enlightenment and beauty that is the Arc of Light. I was not there to be made aware or welcomed as before. No, this time I was there to make a final decision. I had asked for this audience and now I had to decide. A decision that was far more complicated than I ever imagined. Still, I knew I had to move on.

That's when the next Living Video began to play.

The Answer Shines

The video opened with the birth of my grandson, Finn. I saw him take his first breath. It was more glorious than my heavenly surroundings. I was spellbound. I saw his life's light emerge into the world I left behind. I saw him wrapped in a blue striped blanket lying next to Penelope in the hospital. I saw Diane, Alex, Heather, Lucy and Chris all radiant and joyous. Then as the scene changed I saw me, Tom Pauley, sitting in a wheelchair holding Finn. I was aware and talking with some difficulty. I was not a vegetable. The right side of my body was not moving. I was alive and functioning. Obviously, I had chosen to return in this video. I wanted to stay right there watching my recovering self holding Finn, soaking in the wonder of part of me being in his new life, but I had more to see and the scene shifted.

I was motoring in my electric wheelchair toward the end of Huntington Beach pier alone, facing a Category 5 hurricane. Apparently, hyperbole follows me everywhere. I knew instantly this was a metaphor with which I would connect. Perhaps because I was so saddened by the disaster show. Forty-foot palm trees along the shoreline were flattened. Pacific Coast Highway was flooded. Twenty-foot waves were pounding the pier one after another, flooding everything in sight and crushing the buildings both on the pier and on the mainland. The roar of the storm was unbearable. There was nothing but noise and destruction everywhere. Ruby's restaurant was already gone, washed into the sea along with the last quarter of the pier. In a scene even Spielberg couldn't sell, I was totally dry and safe. It was like I was in a force field or time bubble, mitigating the surrounding chaos. I struggled to rise, leave my wheelchair and walk. I knew that I could not walk, but I was doing it just the same. My steps were unsure and tentative, but I strengthened as I walked. It was hard grueling work. Every step, every move- ment was rife with pain. I fell and turned to crawl back to my wheelchair, but the chair was gone. I saw a wave wash it over the side into the torrent of water below. With the help of a piece of wood that floated by I stood up. This too was with great effort. I fell many times in that journey. Once I looked back to see if help was coming. There was nothing to see except water and wind and flying debris. Certainly, no people. I was alone. The pier was now breaking apart from both ends. Something, some unknown force was driving me. I was determined to go forward even if I had to crawl.

I didn't like this Living Video. It generated great anxiety within my essence. I wondered if the anxiety was fueled by guilt for choosing to leave. I was immediately answered.

They spoke clearly:

"There is no guilt in choosing. This is not about what you are leaving behind. It is about your journey should you choose to return. There is more to you than you know, Tom."

The wind and the waves were stronger now. I was safe and dry, not overwhelmed by them, but I certainly felt their effect. I had the feeling others thought I was on a fool's errand. I don't know who the others were since I was alone. Maybe these were my own doubts. I engaged in an absurd venture against an impossibly fierce, overpowering and unrelenting assault. Whatever I hoped to accomplish was doomed from the start. The fact I had not already succumbed in my efforts was in itself a miracle. What counterforce could possibly be strong enough to compel me to take on this insane venture? The swirling winds were ripping concrete and steel from the moorings. Visibility was nearly zero. Massive lightning bolts exploded all around me. I could not see anything. I couldn't hear my own thoughts. Watching this Living Video was difficult, because I felt deserted by everyone. I was compelled to pursue this utter insanity and nobody was there for me. Nobody. I had no one behind me. I thought I could hear Diane's voice once, but the roar of the storm drowned that out, too.

I was alone, weak and lowly in a terribly lonely place. I had no one to comfort me, to love me, to support me. The heaviness of the loss of everything I ever loved was devastating. I was ill equipped for what lay ahead of me. I was following an insane path. The pain of separation, the empty hollow feeling of my imminent failure told me to quit, to give up and welcome the inevitable. Curl into a ball, say I'm sorry and let this moment pass to one more capable.

I was pulled to the edge of hopelessness. Even my last vestige of material support, the wheelchair, had washed away. My entire support system had deserted me. The power of the wind and water smashed me into what was left of the pier again and again, impossibly gaining intensity and finally, bursting the time bubble of protection surrounding me. That's when I did a really crazy thing. I know, right? How could anything get crazier and farther from reality than a paralyzed man navigating a dying pier alone in a Category 5 hurricane? I'm sure you wouldn't get the same Living Video. At least, I pray you don't. There was nothing sane and certainly nothing the least bit fun or comforting about it. My Living Video, my what-if-I-returned scenario, was about to get even crazier.

Shoulder To Shoulder

Tears streaming from my eyes, I forced myself to stand once again against the storm. Without my time bubble protecting me, I threw my piece of wooden flotsam into the sea, my one remaining veneer of material support gone. Discarded like a piece of used Kleenex. Something was driving me. Something I could not see or understand. I managed to stand once again with great difficulty. I was so very cold, afraid and exhausted. I knew my journey was insane. Still, I pushed on. I was forging ahead against all odds in the face of inevitable destruction without any support save some unseen and unexplainable counterforce. What was driving me? I had no idea. Alone with only the invisible counterforce for support, I raised my right arm and right hand. I raised my paralyzed right arm! First, I abandoned my wheelchair to stand and walk in a horrific storm. Then, I threw away the crutch I snagged from the roiling water and withstood the constant and growing violence and continued forward. Now, I raised my paralyzed arm, reached inside my coat on the left side just above my heart and took out a magnificent something, brilliantly colored, amazingly radiant and infinitely compelling. I extended this radiant gift as an offering to the raging storm. Immediately, the gift was ripped from my weakened right hand and blown into the watery abyss. But the gift was not gone. Instantly, it appeared again in my hand. I extended it as before. Again, it was ripped away. Again, it reappeared in my hand. This went on for some time. Offering this amazing gift, having it ripped from my hand and then reappearing.

I focused all my attention on the gift. Hoping to see and understand exactly what the gift was that I held. I quickly understood that I was not allowed to know what the gift was until I made my final choice.

As I watched my reanimated self on the ever shrinking and collapsing pier, I noticed someone crawl from the ocean. She walked next to me offering the same brilliant gift. It was Penelope. The wind blew hers away, too. And hers also returned to her hand. She continued to offer her gift to the storm as I did with similar results. Then, I noticed Diane standing behind me offering the same divinely colored gift achieving the same results. I don't know how long she had been standing there, but it seemed like she'd always been there unseen, supporting my every move. Eventually, more people came. Jillian, Dempsey, Lisa, Bob, Dave, Alex, Heather, Levi, Cherie, Doug, Chris, Joe, Barb, Dean, Mark, Jim, Sherri, Symeon – too many to name. Quickly they came almost faster than I could recognize them. They came first in ones and twos, then in pairs and finally in groups. Each came with the same glowing and brilliantly colored sphere. Each standing shoulder to shoulder with those they didn't know, offering the magnificent gift and having it blown away only to return instantly.

Imperceptibly, at first, the storm began to calm. The waves became smaller, the winds weaker. Miraculously the pier began to reconstruct as the storm weakened. Soon hundreds, then thousands, then millions came bearing the same wondrous gift. Finally, the clouds departed and waters were still. The storm clouds began to dissipate and the sun shone through.

That's when I turned and saw you standing there on that pier. Yes, you who are now reading this book. I saw you on that pier with everyone else. I saw the confidence in your eyes. Weathered and weary, but strong. You were illuminating everything around you with the well-earned confidence that comes from facing a hard, impossible foe and winning. I was so proud to be standing with you. So very, very proud.

I told you earlier I had seen you standing with me. Shoulder to shoulder. You will soon understand how this can be. You will be there on that pier as soon as you receive your Miracle Healing.

Beaming with pride of unity, I rose to a higher vantage point and I could see millions of people just like you across the globe offering the same amazing gift to the storms and fires and deadly chaos raging in their lands. I saw your work everywhere. Everywhere the Chosen Ones grew brighter and stronger. You grew brighter and stronger. You had become a touchstone of abundance and healing. The lands and seas around you flourished from your healing. Every group grew the same way, first one, then more, then multitudes. We were miraculously healing the earth and ourselves, ushering in a world of infinite abundance and healing.

I respect the absolute power and authority of the Supreme Force of All-Creation and His Messengers. I have never deluded myself into believing that I was anything more than a man with certain talents and abilities. I could work for His Cause on earth, but I was not Him. Now, I'm shown this video. I could see that I had been given a wondrous gift. It was a gift that would bring healing to all. A gift I would and must share, a compelling driving counterforce to the problems overwhelming our earth, our lives, our transformational playground.

What was that amazing gift? What could possibly not only calm the plethora of storms destroying the people and the world, but also empower and strengthen so many? Giving them – us a courage and strength we didn't know we had? It was this gift that drove me beyond all human sensibility and good sense to push ahead without any support into that storm of certain catastrophe. The gift I held shown brighter and more beautifully than anything I had ever seen on earth or in the Arc of Light.

The answers came only after I made my final choice. As I watched these relatively few souls – millions out of billions – as I watched this handful of humans stand together and wield a force powerful enough to calm the raging storms destroying us, I realized that this was something I wanted to be part of. It didn't matter if I was the first guy on that pier or the last, I wanted to be there. All my life I have seen the awful things humanity was capable of doing. Like so many others, I felt the pain of knowing wrongs were being committed, atrocities were being allowed to continue without my doing anything about it. Forces beyond my control were unduly limiting my abundance and the abundance of others. I was being offered the chance to do something to bring peace and healing to the world. I had waited for this, for however long I've been alive on this planet.

I Had To Go Back

My Miracle Healing appeared in the instant I decided to return. It was accompanied by the divine equivalent of a sonic boom. Startling and full of wonder, it demanded my interest. I watched in awe as it burst through the wall of the Arc of Light like it was coming from another universe. The Living Video of the world healing was still playing in the background. A strong loving voice of Supreme Authority and Power resonated though me:

"It will be long and difficult, but you will have a full and complete recovery."

An ocean of the most magnificent healing colors imaginable instantly overwhelmed me. They came in waves. First a shorter opening volley of loving healing energy, then a longer even more powerful barrage of pure, unadulterated Miracle Healing. They flooded my being and dominated my senses. They were radiant beyond words, an infinite rainbow of colors, beautiful without measure. They were strong and gentle, compelling and protective, pure, sweet, satisfying, loving, comforting, empowering and infinitely healing. A healing, which finally came to rest in my heart as a magnificent, rainbow colored sphere, a sphere that shone with the intensity of billions and trillions of stars.

I was bathed in absolute joy.

I know I'm not doing the whole experience justice. I'm just throwing words at you trying to convey that experience. Words alone cannot accurately portray the feeling and sense of amazing well-being that surged through me. Know that the restorative and healing energy radiating through my essence from this infinite rainbow of indescribably brilliant colors was beyond description. As I basked for what seemed like an eternity in this pure joy, I heard the voice of Supreme Authority and Power once again:

"This powerful healing is enabled by Us. Given to you by those who love Us. It is given as a trust. Not to keep, but to share. Go back and continue your work. Take Our message of this miracle to the people of the world. They are expecting it. Once they hear this message they will send this healing to you. They can only send this healing after they hear your message. We know you understand this, Tom. Help them understand this also.

"Show them by your example how very powerful they are. Show them how they can send you this healing. Show them how they can heal themselves and others they love.

"This is how you received your healing. This is how others will receive the healing which they have for so long prayed for Us to send. This is how you and all those who desire Our Goodness take part in healing your kind.

"Share the message, Tom. You have spent your entire earthly experience learning skills that would prepare you for this work. This is your mission, Tom.

Once others hear this message they will join in the healing."

How Your Miracle Healing Works

CHAPTER 14

Ice Cream

When I need to process something as intense and impacting as the previous chapter – I go to the beach. When I don't have any interest in painting or writing, or doing any of the things I usually do to process important information – I go to the beach. When I need to solve a problem or simply clear my mind of all the doubt and clutter life naturally brings – I go to the beach. I go to the beach and sit for an hour revitalizing my mind and soul with the amazing healing qualities of nature. I don't talk to anyone. I don't do anything except sit quietly and let our precious transformational playground do the rest.

This morning I went to my favorite spot in Heisler Park in Laguna Beach, California. I sat on my favorite bench on a cliff over-looking the Pacific Ocean. It gives me a 180-degree view of an absolutely gorgeous seascape. On the right and seventy feet below, the ocean smashes into a rocky and sculptured shoreline. The cliff is beautifully landscaped with a wide variety of plant life accented with an abundance of palm trees with few prickly pear cacti for texture. In spring and summer a visual banquet of flowers welcome all those who come to celebrate another day in paradise. The fragrance of the flowers mixed with the fresh sea air calls weary travelers to a daily feast of healing.

The flourish of the waves hitting the rocks and the beach is so clearing that a feeling of renewal resonates through my body like an electric surge. The waves start breaking about seventy-five or a hundred yards before getting to the small sheltered beach on the right, so the effect is quite dramatic. The view from above is spectacular. Many folks stop to take a quick picture with their cell phones hoping to capture their moment in paradise. For me that's not enough. I prefer to sit and experience the moment. A giant date palm stands in the middle of this view separating the two sides. On the left there are fewer rocky outcroppings to slow the force of the waves crashing to the beach. This side is louder and seems more active, more action packed, more powerful, I guess. It is every bit as beautiful as the right, a little rougher, perhaps. Less controlled. More like it might have been twenty, fifty, a hundred million years ago. It's not, of course, but the thought stimulates my imagination. Sometimes, I imagine dinosaurs coming out of the ocean to warm themselves in this very spot. This is the side that generally draws my attention.

Just five days away from St. Valentine's Day, and the sun is already sending its bounty of warming rays to generate another year of new growth, new challenges, new beginnings. As I sit there inhaling the abundance and the wealth of healing the Universe has provided, my mind jumps from one problem to another. Trying not to think of anything, I think of so many things. This stage ends soon enough and my jumble of problems and thoughts dissipate with the morning fog. I simply sit and enjoy the beauty all around me. A flock of seven brown pelicans glide by just below my eye level. They are not looking for food or going anywhere in particular. They are doing the same thing I am, kicking back and delighting in the wealth of nature. Before long my problems have evaporated completely. Simple solutions seem to pop into my head while I watch another brown pelican join the flock as they round the point on the right. Without my doing anything, answers and solutions fill my mind, leaving me happy, refreshed and eager to get back to work.

Nature Heals Your Soul

Now, if you don't have a beach to go to, then go somewhere else. Go to nature if you can. Somewhere where you can sit or walk undisturbed for a while and let your mind reboot. Go to the mountains and feel what it feels like to see the top of the world. Maybe you'll get to watch the snow fall or melt into a stream of sweet, clear water. Go to the desert. Sit and take in the miracle of life persisting despite the arid conditions, watch lizards skitter across the ground and buzzards patrol the sky. Go to a lake and sit on a pier and watch the fish jump as the sun plays on water. Or go to a park, smell the fresh air. If it's spring you might even be treated to the courting rituals of the birds and squirrels. Or in the Midwest you can sit on the fender of your car and watch the wind create waves across a field of green July corn. An hour in nature is like ice cream after a rich meal. It clears your mental and emotional palate. Take your time. Let your doubt and worries evaporate. Don't do anything. Don't think about anything. Just sit and enjoy the natural beauty and wonder God has given you. Soothe and heal your troubled soul by doing absolutely nothing at all. An hour in nature is a mental recharge so powerful it borders on magical.

You deserve a break. Miracle Healing is not to be taken lightly. Go to nature. Take a break and refresh your spirit. I am going to show you how to send a Miracle Healing into the past, back on the early morning hours of March 29, 2009. You will want your wits about you. Time travel and Miracle Healing are pretty impressive things to do. Individually, they are impressive, but both at the same time, wow!

Now, that's something to write home about.

CHAPTER 15
Profound Discovery

In 1964 Irish Physicist, James Bell, made what fellow scientists have called the most profound discovery in science. He laid to rest the confusion and disbelief that had raged in scientific circles since the dawn of the 20th century, and still persists today among the general public and, ironically, among a few scientists. Do we live in a physical reality or a quantum reality? Bell proved once and for all that we live in a quantum reality. A discovery that has incredibly far ranging effects, but we'll get to that later. His experiment does not make scientists or laymen gasp with astonishment and turn cartwheels upon hearing it. The heart of the experiment is an inequality hidden in the math. If you're interested, you can read a good description of that experiment and others mentioned in this chapter in Dean Radin's book, Entangled Minds: Extrasensory Experiences in a Quantum Reality. It is a fascinating and mind expanding book. I even understood most of it. From this inequality in the math Bell was able to derive his theorem:

"No physical theory of local hidden variables can ever reproduce all of the predictions of quantum mechanics." I know that doesn't have you turning cartwheels either, does it? Penelope and I came up with a non-scientific explanation, which is much easier to digest. We like it. "You cannot explain infinity with finite terms."

Regardless of the wording, the shockwaves of his discovery have only begun to roll. Bell's theorem of inequality can be a little obtuse for laymen, but for the vast majority of today's scientific community it is proof positive we live in a quantum reality, making it the most profound discovery in science. A discovery that has a life changing impact on all of us.

Such a powerful and fundamental change in understanding how the world works is difficult to accept, even for scientists. If you think you have trouble accepting all the new ideas and concepts you face every day, you are in good company. Since the discovery of quantum theory, scientists worldwide had worked overtime to prove it was wrong. Debunk the whole concept. Not because it is good science to prove any theory. No, it had already been proven countless times. In scientific circles refusing to accept quantum theory would be like apple growers refusing to accept gravity. I'm sure the mere mention of the possibility of this mass rejection would have Sir Isaac Newton spinning in his sarcophagus. Yet, scientists everywhere simply refused to accept the most proven theory in the history of humankind. At a worldwide scientific conference in the early 1950's one renowned physicist presented a paper postulating the effects of quantum field theory when applied to our everyday lives. He was booed off stage and blackballed from the scientific community worldwide. He never worked in his field again.

Quantum theory is the reason we have computers, the Internet, modern cars and television. Why would highly intelligent men and women oppose such a powerful advance in human knowledge? Why would those who sought to uncover hidden truths about how the world works deny something that opened so many new doors? I believe they refused to accept quantum theory because the implications are so staggering, so impossible to accept. Everything they thought they knew about how the world works would have to be questioned. Years of their hard work would be open to doubt and their work, the solutions they had discovered using their logical minds defined them. It meant they were wrong. It meant they had to rethink the fundamental pillars of reality, as they understood them. Because quantum theory clearly says reality is much bigger than it seems, and most of it is invisible. Invisible? Forces we cannot see, smell, feel, taste or hear affect us?

Impossible!

These were scientists, not priests. They worked with tangibles, not intangibles. Not spooky happenings at a distance. Everything they believed true and accurate had to be re-examined? This couldn't be right. Their life's work would have been a sham. The logic they lived by demanded they were frauds. The shame they felt must have been enormous. Naturally, they rejected what they saw as the cause of their difficulty. Quantum theory had to be a mistake…some weird unexplainable anomaly.

Albert Einstein couldn't get his head around it. The man whose *Special Theory of Relativity* (published in 1906) opened the door to the possibility of messages and matter traveling backward in time. Albert Einstein, the grandfather of plausible time-travel, said that if quantum mechanics was correct, then the world was crazy. Well, Albert, welcome to the insane asylum. Because James Bell's theorem of inequalities proved we live not in the linear cause and effect reality we think we do, but in a seemingly unpredictable quantum reality where time can travel backwards, effect can come before cause and ordinary human minds hold a power inconceivable until now. Certainly, that would scare the living daylights out of anybody.

Don't get down on yourself if this quantum view of how things can work in our world doesn't feel self-evident. You are in good company. It takes some getting used to. Neils Bohr, Nobel Laureate and the father of atomic physics said, "If you are not shocked when you first come across quantum theory, you cannot possibly have understood it." *Reality is much bigger than it seems and most of it is invisible.* Unfortunately, you cannot invalidate truth because it takes some understanding, nor because you don't particularly like the implications it has for your life.

Truth is truth and truth will out.

When you woke up this morning you knew tomorrow never comes. You knew to make the most of today because you will never get a second chance. You knew that you couldn't cry over yesterday because it is long gone, old news, history. You knew you could not change the past. You knew that time was constantly marching forward. That what happens today can never be undone. These axioms reflect the bedrock of how we understood the basic matrix of this temporal time zone. If we didn't have a practical understanding of how the world works, we simply couldn't function day in and day out. If, for example, we didn't know that red means stop, green means go and yellow means go very, very fast, traffic would get a whole lot messier than it is now. Still, it's shocking for anyone to learn the axioms we lived by were not completely true, and that they must adjust their understanding of how life works.

Oh, most of the time these axioms are true, but they are not absolute. And that simple distinction, that inequality, opens a door of opportunity for you and me that is worth more than all the gold in Fort Knox. More importantly, it opens the door to a level of healing unknown on earth until now. You can go back and repair mistakes from the past. You can enjoy an effect that has not yet been caused. You can raise your own level of healing and abundance. And you can raise the consciousness of billions of humans you have never even met all at the same time. All from the privacy of your living room, no less.

One Step Back

Back in my movie script writing days I had my first meaningful experience with a psychologist and applied quantum theory. Therapy is practically a requirement for working with Hollywood. If you didn't need it before, you'll certainly need it after. In the course of my therapy, my shrink regressed me to various ages, so that I could simply hug and comfort my younger self. By doing this she claimed that I would heal the hurt I experienced in the past and by doing so eliminate the cause of my anger today. It was a very common therapy technique, I was told. At first, I thought this was about the dumbest thing I'd ever heard. *You can't go back in time. You cannot change the past.* She said she would hypnotize me and take me back to meet my nine-year-old self. I could then assure him that the divorce his parents were going through was not his fault. That it was natural to be angry about the loss of his family unit. That he would grow up to be a strong, loving and productive man with a family of his own. Then I would hug the boy and absorb him into my adult self.

I was reluctant to go through the effort at first because I believed the whole concept was flawed from the start. It even took her a couple of weeks to convince me to try. I might also have been a tad bit concerned she would plant post-hypnotic suggestions and one day I'd start clucking like a chicken for no apparent reason, but I'd never admit that. I was having issues with authority figures, however, and they weren't getting better.

Finally, I agreed to try. An amazing thing happened. It worked. When I went into the deep hypnotic state I actually did meet and talk to my younger self. He told me he was very afraid. He didn't know what would become of him. He was sure the divorce was his fault and he was terrified he couldn't take Dad's place. We carried on a full conversation until he was finished releasing his pain. I reassured and comforted him, then spread my arms wide accepting him into my heart. It was a marvelous feeling, very satisfying, very happy, very fulfilling. Not only was I helping someone in emotional pain, but that someone was me. Without further suggestion he ran forward, hugged me and merged into my present adult self. If I hadn't been in a therapist's office I would have thought I needed to have my head examined. When I came out of the trance I felt something I hadn't felt for a long time – peace.

Many Steps Forward

You absolutely cannot move ahead with your life when you are mired in the past. By not forgiving your past, you have locked yourself in a prison of self. In the classic sense, we simply cannot be in two places at the same time in this matrix. An unresolved pain from your past will keep you stuck exactly where and when you were hurt. Or where you hurt someone else for that matter, since there is no separation between you and the one you hurt.

We are all one. There is no timeline in life. Time and space are permanently fused together. If you were injured yesterday and didn't forgive those involved and resolve the issue in your mind, then you are injured still. When you forgive someone it is you who benefits the most. You receive a direct and immediate healing, not the other guy. The unresolved pain you experienced at twelve, twenty-two or forty-two is still hurting you today. As my shrink used to say, "Under anger and resentment lies fear and under fear lies pain. Eliminate the pain and you eliminate the anger and resentment." I guarantee you that your life becomes a whole lot less stressful and far more successful in everything you do. Making you a happier and healthier being. Until you face up to your injury and resolve your buried pain, it will never leave you alone. Anger and resentment will bubble up through the filter of your personality, and cause you to make decisions and take actions which are not in your own best interests, and which propagate exactly the opposite of the good you seek to create in your life.

Unresolved anger and resentment are intrinsic to scarcity consciousness. Without them scarcity consciousness is one step closer to extinction. Defining yourself within a shroud of negativity is downright dangerous. You can have and do anything in this life. Even heal long buried pain. Holding on to the garbage of yesterday invites grave peril into your life and your future.

One session didn't cure me of all my issues, of course. Nor will it cure you. New stuff presents itself all the time and needs to be dealt with. Eventually, this season of my life passed. *There is a time for everything. A season for every activity under the heavens.* Ecclesiastes 3:1. You can only effect change when you are ready to do it. You must also process the change and make it part of your consciousness. It took me a while to understand and grow comfortable with what I had done in these exercises. I traveled backward through time and changed my life forever. I never felt that gnawing anxiety over my parents' divorce after that day. *Reality was much bigger than it seems and most of it is invisible.* I had changed the present by changing the past. I almost felt guilty. Like I had broken some Newtonian Law. I know psychologists would say I didn't go anywhere because all my selves are contained within me. And my regression simply allowed me to resolve an internal conflict. I saw something greater. I saw a door open. I saw a path to do what others said couldn't be done. I made a quantum leap in my understanding of how life worked. I saw myself as a real life time-traveler. I found healing for my present day problem by traveling to own my past and comforting my younger self. I applied quantum theory directly to my life. I did this using only the power of my mind to reach into the quantum field. I had elevated my consciousness. Although I didn't understand it in those terms yet. This was my first experience using Quantum Theory.

I am eternally grateful for the release this simple exercise provided me. As you will be once you experience the peace it brings.

Elevating your consciousness is an inevitable and never-ending process. If you resist growth and change, you will increase your pain and discomfort. Because that keeps you stuck in the same test over and over again until you learn the lesson. How can you move forward until each lesson is accepted? Your growth is progressive. You can't run until you know how to walk, right? Regardless of how difficult it might become once you deliberately seek to elevate your consciousness by accepting your lessons as they come, your life experiences will become more pleasant, less stressful and advance you on your path more quickly.

Of course, resisting is second nature to folks like me.

Rich Beyond My Wildest Dreams

Near the turn of the 21st century, still struggling to find that elusive pot of gold I knew was mine, I met someone who introduced me to another new level of understanding of how things worked in our space-time matrix. Her name was Marilyn and she helped me elevate my consciousness by leaps and bounds. Penelope and I talk about her in our book *I'm Rich Beyond My Wildest Dreams. I am. I am. I am.* Marilyn gave us a great system that allowed us to enrich our lives using the power of Universal Laws like the Law of Attraction, the Law of Multiplication and the Law of Compensation. She gave us a simple system that allowed us to ask and receive anything we wanted in life. This system was not based on hard work and long hours. It didn't matter what your nationality, race, gender, sexual preference, experience, education, religion or lack of religion was. It didn't matter whether you were rich or poor. It didn't even matter whether you believed the system would work or not. The only thing that mattered was doing it, which took only a few minutes a day, detailing specifically what you wanted. Oh, and your total investment was a 79-cent wide-ruled, spiral bound notebook. Who wouldn't want that? That system is the very definition of a great low cost investment. Who wouldn't gladly seek and accept such powerful insight?

You guessed it. Me, of course; I resisted.

I avoided Marilyn for almost six months after I met her because she charged for her service. Imagine that, actually charging for your work. Really, her radical ideas about the universe scared the devil out of me. I knew deep within my being that hard work was the key to success. I knew good investments were expensive, Lord knows I bought into more than a few. I knew there must be a catch to something as radical as she proposed. Surely there was a catch and an expensive one at that. I wasn't about to give Marilyn any of my hard earned money to hear her pitch. Until she told my wife to tell me she could triple my commissions. Now that got my attention. That was something I could investigate. That was something I could use.

The elevation of your consciousness invariably begins with your desire to improve your living conditions or your health or your love life. This is natural because you are human. Who gets really excited about the evolution of their consciousness? "Whoopee! I have elevated myself. Let's all go out and celebrate." Where's the profit in that? No, you want to improve your lot in life. You want a personal benefit you can see, hear, smell, taste or touch. That's what calls to you. That's where you invest your time. That's how you imagine you will grow stronger and richer. What you do not as easily recognize is that all those human desires for an improved lot in life are only a veiled need to grow and expand your consciousness.

This is your real gain. This is the prize you desperately want. This is the hidden profit you ultimately seek.

The secret to success in the human experience is not hard work. Because no matter how hard you work you can only achieve as much as your consciousness allows you to achieve. Markets rise and fall. Products come in and out of vogue. Natural disasters affect the food supply. Children grow up and leave home to follow their own dreams. People grow old and die. Nothing in this time-space matrix guarantees you success. No matter what you do or where you invest your time, the natural course of events is waiting to lay havoc to your dreams of earthly success. Of course, wanting those dreams, wanting to improve your lot in life is not only natural, but also a very important driving force in your life. Because wanting things opens the door to growth and expansion. As you ask and receive you expand and elevate your consciousness. As a result everything that is important comes to you. Everything that improves your life comes to you. Everything that makes your life meaningful and gives you satisfaction comes to you. They all come by means over which you have no control, simply because you ask. No chasing required.

This was my second experience with the quantum side of reality. I did receive all the things I asked for within three weeks. And I had an exhaustive list. How was that possible, if you must first raise your consciousness to attract the things you asked for? I wasn't trying to raise my consciousness. I was asking for stuff, not growth. I wanted to improve my lot in life. I wanted material well-being.

We live in a quantum reality and sometimes the cause comes after the effect. I asked for things and got them. The cause that allowed me to attract them, an elevated consciousness, came later because of my experience with having the stuff. The cause came after the effect.

You may indeed work long hard hours, but that is absolutely not the source of your good fortune. Expanding and elevating your consciousness is the only ultimate guarantee for human success.

Marilyn was right. The system she gave me did triple my commissions. Armed with that system my family blossomed. After years of chasing success it found me. I built a happy successful life filled with big houses, new cars and an international business. My business was booming and it was practically running itself. All of which are things I asked for. Great opportunities would jump into my lap. My mind was overflowing with great ideas; all this because of a simple system to ask and receive. Not because I worked harder or longer. The secret of my success was quite obvious to me. Or so I thought.

Ask and Buddha provides.

Overnight it seemed, I moved my family to a house close to the beach and we started enjoying life a whole lot more than ever before. After we started enjoying the benefits of using our new system, Penelope and I asked to make selling come faster and easier. A simple request because we were again working long hard hours cold calling tech businesses to sell them advertising on a tiny new website. I must mention that in 1996 all websites were new and most were large and well-funded. Small was the exception. It was the beginning of the commercialization of the Internet. We were starting with two strikes against us. Our competition were sites bankrolled by huge public corporations with a staff of experienced tech savvy salesmen. Penelope and I were working on commission, hoping and praying we hit a homerun before we got strike three because we had no funding. We had no support. We needed an easier way.

Ask and you shall receive.

A Revolutionary Course Of Action

We discovered a system that allowed us to reach prospects anywhere, any time without much effort. We went from struggling to thriving. Our first year using this system we outsold our biggest competitor and their scores of experienced salesmen. We talk about this in our on-line course, *Quantum Selling, A*

Revolutionary Course Of Action. The secret to the system was a simple process for accessing the quantum field and connecting to anyone in the world, whether we knew them or not, anywhere, anytime. It was and remains a singularly powerful and effective system for connecting to the universal consciousness. Naturally, we discovered this versatile new human technology because of our desire to improve our lot in life.

We became wonderfully successful, practically overnight. What we didn't realize until much later was that all our human success was really a graphic interface, a human theater for the bigger change in us, our elevated consciousness. We had been introduced to the Law of Connection. We recognized in the most human terms possible, profit and loss, that we could connect very effectively with other humans we didn't know. The awareness that we must connect to them would come later. At first, we thought that connecting to all humankind was essential because it brought us success. We thought of it as an inexpensive and very effective advertising and promotion campaign. The more we connected the more sales we made.

What we didn't realize was that we were elevating others by connecting with their consciousness. Since it was and remains the ultimate human desire to elevate your consciousness, our work in the Portal drove our sales. Not because we were great salesmen. Not because we were selling the world's greatest discovery since buggy whips; no, it was because the Quantum Selling protocols touched their hearts and elevated their consciousness. Our great success was made possible because of our unconditional and open connection of pure intent. Much like a connection you might have with someone you love and in whom you retain no hidden intention for harm, abuse or self-interest.

We were open and completely honest in the Portal. We did not try to persuade, we only informed. That openness of pure intent is the super highway to raising the consciousness of others and as a result attracting more of the good you desire for yourself. Once you elevate your consciousness the more powerful you become and the faster you attract the good you desire. Of course, elevating others also elevates your consciousness. Which means you attract even more of what you desire, faster. Definitely a win/win scenario. Raising up others puts you on the fast track to the peace and the infinite abundance you deeply desire.

At first, the idea of total openness seemed counter to my idea of success, which I still saw as stacking up enough gold to feel safe and protected against all obstacles. Still, the more we opened the Portal, our term for using the Quantum Selling system to access the quantum field, the greater our success grew. Who fights success? My life became a living example of rags to riches without great effort. I was living my dream. We all were. This was our first experience with intentionally and deliberately using applied quantum theory in our lives.

I decided that I was on the runway to my ultimate success. I had the wings that could carry me to the pinnacle of my material desires. All I had to do was go into the Portal every day and welcome my good when it arrived. Spread the word. Sell those Courses. Count the income. I had found Sugar Mountain and I was heading for the top. I planned to go on doing what I was doing forever. I had no way of knowing the end was coming. *There is a time for everything. A season for every activity under the heavens.* The season for my growth using Quantum Selling only was quickly coming to an end. I was about to elevate my consciousness again whether I liked it or not.

Long before I could even write Quantum Selling I had to accept the mantle of a conduit for divine information. That meant I agreed to be a test dummy. I would be given tests and difficulties along with solutions you could apply in your life. I agreed to pass that knowledge on to you. Until I agreed, the information for *Quantum Selling: A Revolutionary Course Of Action* simply would not flow from my fingers. My attempts were doomed to failure. I spent a year trying unsuccessfully to write that course even though I'd been using it successfully for the better part of a decade. I did not consciously want nor seek that mantle, but it was mine to accept or refuse. I made a great decision.

A new period of my growth materialized out of the Great Recession and my stroke. Again I did not see those triggers as a benefit any more than I saw them ushering in a new period of growth and understanding of applied quantum theory. The big picture was simply not available to this mortal human. Clarity is the great gift of hindsight.

What is now clear to me is that I had received an opportunity for a new level of growth and expansion. I was given a doorway to a radically higher level of abundance. A level of abundance that transcends fancy cars and big houses. A level of abundance that elevates your understanding of security and well-being. A level of abundance that makes your life more relevant, more complete and infinitely more satisfying. I was given the opportunity to accept a new level of abundance that heals the very essence of Who I Am.

My opportunity came in the form of a mission and a gift, which I now offer you.

You Are Powerful Beyond Measure

I now understand and accept that my fear of who I really am is why I had so much difficulty writing this book. Ironic, isn't it? My reluctance to receive my gift was the very reason I needed to receive it. That realization came the day I finished many of the previous chapters. I had written in circles for six months, trying desperately to avoid admitting to myself and to you the mission I'd been given. I risked everything – my family, my friendships, my wealth, my well-being, my home, my business, my future and my health by refusing to accept who I was. What a fool I can be! I honestly believed I wasn't good enough, smart enough and talented enough to do the job God had given me. Who am I to question God?! I was terrified that I, Tom Pauley, was powerful beyond measure. That I could say unto the mountain go into the sea, and it would go as His Holiness Christ said we could do over two thousand years ago.

I was refusing my own God-given greatness.

We are not on this planet to live lives of quiet desperation. We were not chosen for the earthly experience so we could while away our precious few minutes here perpetuating a scarcity consciousness.

NO!!!

We were born to greatness! I was born to greatness. You were born to greatness. Greatness cannot be thrust upon you. It may take an activating incident to wake you up, but that was planned long before you ever got here. That you are here in this moment, in humanity's greatest time of need, attests to your greatness. It means you are here to help bring about the next major shift in the evolution of humankind. That's pretty great, right? The

Ultimate Source of All Knowledge wouldn't choose the second team for that job, now would She?

We were given membership in the human community so we could improve our own consciousness and the universal consciousness in the process. Each and every one of us was given a unique and important path to walk. We can't possibly walk someone else's path and no one else can walk ours. We were given the power to ask and receive. The power to choose and reap the consequences. The power to try and fail and succeed. The power to open doors that none have opened before. The power to embody the Infinite Possibility of Creation, extending and expanding our lives and the lives of those with whom we share this blue marble in space and time.

Like it or not you are the most powerful force in your own life. You are already capable of great change and healing. I know. I've seen you do it. I'm living proof of your greatness and power. Now even if you don't accept my proof, or you breeze over that statement out of feigned humility or fear that it might just be true, then stop and think about this for a minute. You and only you can ask and receive the things you want in this life. That's no small feat. No matter how rich or poor you are, only you can realize your deepest desires. All you have to do is ask and willingly receive. That alone is huge!

You and only you have the power to create the life you came here to live. You have the power to connect to and influence those around you. You are the most powerful force in your universe next to God. Not gamma rays, world leaders, or the latest technology. Certainly not the world economy or the price of eggs and gasoline. You are not an accident! You were chosen. **You are here because you are powerful beyond measure.** You have the unrestrained power to ask God personally for the things you want in your life with every expectation of receiving them. This verifiable, God-given gift of Ask and Receive only scratches the surface of your powers.

Now consider that you have powers you do not yet realize you have. You have powers with which you can reach out and sell anything to anyone anywhere on the planet, whether you are a salesman or not. Powers that can help you find your divine complement. Powers that keep you connected to those you love and the entirety of the human family, regardless of where they are or how they feel about you. Or how you feel about them. We have already demonstrated the effectiveness of these powers with *Quantum Selling*. We know this as a fact, as do our many students.

Now consider this:

I know for a fact you have even greater powers. You have the power to reach into the past and alter the present. You have the power to reach, inform and empower those whom you do not know, have never met, who live in another country, speak a different language and who may hate the ground you walk on. Wait, it gets even better! I know without a shred of doubt that you have the power to create Miracle Healing and raise the dead.

Because I have seen you do these things.

You are the reason I'm here today. The reason I'm alive today. The reason I can talk, walk and write. The reason I'm no longer paralyzed. The reason the dead spot in my brain moved off my brain stem. The reason I could recover from the unrecoverable. I have seen what you can do. You can't hide from me. I know who you are. You are an amazingly powerful being beyond anything you can imagine.

I am going to show you how to wield that power to an even greater degree. I'm going to walk you through how you can access a Miracle Healing for yourself. How you can extend that Miracle Healing to your loved ones and others you don't even know, but who as fellow members of our human community hold great influence over your healing and your abundance. How you can send your Miracle Healing to me while I was in the Presence of the Generous One back in the early morning hours of March 29, 2009. But first, I have one more story you absolutely must hear. Well, maybe two.

I must caution you. When I first told Penelope these stories she was speechless for a good two minutes, which may be a record for her. Her mouth was open, her lips moved, but no words came out. She has worked with quantum reality since the end of last century. If she was shocked to her core, I wonder what your reaction might be? Put your Mickey Mouse ears on, because you are about to enter a real magic kingdom in our own time-space matrix, which we lovingly refer to as the quantum side.

Oh, and remember you live in a quantum reality. There's one thing you can always be assured of:

Reality Is Much Bigger Than It Seems And Most Of It Is Invisible

CHAPTER 16

Deliverance

Energy is everything. Everything is energy.

In our time-space matrix, our transformational playground, everything is made of energy. You, me, butterflies, shark teeth, the sun, the moon, your liver, your brain, your ideas, your thoughts, your hopes and dreams, your emotions, your communication, the community in which you live, visible light, brick walls, up quarks, down quarks, strange quarks – even your consciousness is constructed entirely, solely and exclusively of energy. What we perceive as reality is no more than just a bunch of atoms moving very, very fast to create whatever it is to which we are giving our attention. Of course, those atoms are made up of energy, too. This world is merely an illusion.

Wait!

You've heard this all before, haven't you? It's a common refrain among those who have been working hard to help you find your way to your highest potential. Teachers, preachers, coaches, trainers, mentors, writers. We have consistently told you that what your mind can imagine, you can have.

We here at RichDreams.com have told you that creating a vision of the things you desire is the fast track to possessing those very things in your life. That you can, in the privacy of your home, use your mind to create your own reality. The fact that this process works, however, does not do much to help you recognize the illusionary nature of your world. Even the most ardent proponent of this unreal world theory is going to feel searing pain when she slams her bare toes into the wooden footing of a bedpost. Or when he slices his finger with a paring knife. Einstein once said, "Reality is an illusion, albeit a persistent one."

The fact is, we are not supposed to easily recognize the transitory and illusionary nature of this world on a day-to-day basis. We are here to make real choices with real consequences, so we can experience how our choices affect others and ourselves. That's somewhat mitigated if we could find a way to slip between the atoms in a brick wall and avert the impediment on our path. We'll leave walking through walls to those comic book movies – for now anyway. Who knows what tomorrow may bring?

My reason for bringing all this up is to set the stage for a better understanding of how information travels in our world. As you remember, James Bell proved that we live in a quantum reality, not a strictly physical one. So how does that work exactly? Then on a more personal level, how does that affect your day-to-day life? What does any of this have to do with your making a better income, finding the love of your life or getting more of the things you want and need to become who you came here to become?

To completely understand that process, we must fully comprehend and accept the fact that your actions affect much more than you know. Your actions, including the action of elevating your own consciousness, like everything else, are composed entirely of energy. We all know that energy affects energy. Proven by the grade school demonstration of activating a second tuning fork by touching it to another already vibrating tuning fork. What you may not be clear on is that energy can travel great distances through brick walls across oceans, mountains and through our space-time matrix to other dimensions.

We have been telling you that by elevating your consciousness you can and will elevate all humankind, creating a richer, more abundant life for you to live now and in the future.

Going into a meditative state and going back to heal your younger self is good, as far as it goes. It demonstrates how the energy of your actions today can affect your own energy in the past and in so doing heal your present. It certainly does not explain how you can send a miracle healing back to me March 29, 2009, thereby creating a Miracle Healing for me and by the very nature of our time-space matrix, a Miracle Healing for you and all that you love, which is what I have been asked to explain. Let's start by talking about the interconnected nature of life on this planet.

My family's hometown for many years was Cook, Nebraska, population 315 according to the sign on the highway. But it's Nebraska, so who knows to which census it refers. I never lived there personally. My folks moved there long after I'd left home. But I have great memories of going back to visit before my mom and step-dad passed and everybody seemed to scatter to the four winds. I remember the great barbeques at my ex-step brother-in-law, Bob's, house, when he was married to my first cousin Barbara. Roger, my second cousin Peggy's husband, cooked the ribs or tri-tip to mouth-watering perfection using his secret marinade, which I found out later, was a can of Coke. Occasionally, we'd eat at the Yacht Club. Great prime steaks! Oh, the Yacht Club was the original name on the Budweiser sign of the town's only restaurant, bar and arcade. The sign was shot out by kids with .22's years ago, but the name stuck. Last time I was there you could still see some of the "Y" on one side, if you looked real hard. My nephews, Mike and Teddy, Bob and Barbara's only son, still live there, but the rest of my mix and match family has pretty much left for greener pastures. Yes, I have great memories of family, but that's not what I remember most about Cook.

What I remember most is how fast word got around. How interconnected they were. My nephew, David, had a plaque in his kitchen that read: *There's not much to see in a small town, but what you hear makes up for it.* It was amazing. We'd just get to town and everybody would know what we were wearing and what we drove. Within minutes, it seemed! We were those "California folks."

At one point Teddy and his then girlfriend, Angie, wanted to buy the old "Cook Mansion." A manse it was not. It was a long vacant and drafty 19th century Victorian farmhouse that happened to be on the only hill in town. But you could see it from the covered bridge on Main Street, Nebraska's one and only covered bridge, I must add. Andrew Cook, the original owner of the town site, built that house. So, I guess you could call it the Cook Mansion. Anyway, it seemed the whole town knew about their intentions fifteen minutes after they agreed to get married there and Bob agreed to cosign their loan. In fact, I left Bob's house to pick up my son, Alex, when Teddy came to ask Bob for his signature. It was probably only ten minutes later when Penelope asked directions from an eighty-year-old man who didn't know any of us. We were getting directions because Alex was supposed to be across from "the church." The trouble was this little country town had five churches and one church museum all on the same street. Church attendance is a really big deal in Nebraska. Anyway, the old guy told Penelope that Ted and Angie were buying the old house and getting married there in the spring. Bob had made getting married a stipulation of signing only minutes earlier because the kids were reluctant to make that little bitty commitment. How could the old man already know?

OK, no big deal. Word travels fast in a small town. Everybody knows that. What you may not know is that this phenomenon demonstrates much more than the effects of gossip.

Beyond Gossip

Since everything in our matrix is made entirely of energy, the way we distinguish a calf's liver from a sunflower or a mountain lion is by their frequency. Humans share a common frequency. That's how we know they are humans and not snakes. Well, sometimes that distinction is a little difficult to make, but that's simply a matter of scarcity consciousness in action and a story for another venue. Since all humans resonate at the same frequency it is not a big stretch to understand how you can pass your fine tuned frequency, your elevated consciousness, to another human just by touching them spiritually. Just like what happens when you touch a resonating tuning fork to another one. The second tuning fork starts resonating, instantly. It's the same for human beings. When you resonate at a higher frequency, every-one you touch will resonate at a higher frequency. The difference is you do not have to touch them on the physical plain to pass your elevated frequency along. You don't have to share the same beliefs or the same language. You don't have to share the same country or time zone. You don't have to share the same degree of education, the same economic class or the same love of sports teams. None of that matters. You can touch them through your interconnectedness. This is merely a tangible demonstration of the Universal Law of Connection.

Oh, for future reference, some scientists call this phenomenon quantum entanglement.

In a small town like Cook, there is less diversity than larger groups such as all Nebraskans, all North Americans, or all people reading this book. Cook has a more concentrated frequency system, which makes the connections more transparent. All groups must operate under a specific energy or frequency in order to stay aligned: small towns, schools, churches, the film industry, dance clubs, little league baseball, the world series, the world economy, space exploration. They all have a specific energy alignment. It is how they are drawn together. Those specific energies attract the members to the group. The communication in small groups is simply more apparent. It is vital to the success of the individual members of these groups that they stay current on all information pertaining to that group. Therefore the energy of these individuals is entangled on a quantum level. It is like they have posted an alert filter in their invisible, spiritual network of interconnections to be notified immediately when such information becomes available.

The amazing phenomenon at work here is that the individuals within the group are notified immediately on a spiritual hotline, faster than anyone can pick up a telephone. They certainly know something important is happening long before they hear the words spoken. We experience this phenomenon in our daily lives all the time. Have you ever been delayed from leaving your home on time? Maybe you couldn't find your keys? While you are looking for them the phone rings and it turns out to be a call you wanted or needed to take. Maybe the phone rings and immediately someone's name or face pops into your mind? And sure enough that's who it is. Maybe you're awakened in the middle of the night knowing someone close to you is in distress or pain. Mothers often feel this connection quite strongly with their children. These are all examples of interconnectedness or quantum entanglement.

Now we recognize and accept this phenomenon in our own lives when it affects those close to us. Is it such a stretch to accept that that same interconnection exists among all human beings? Friend, foreigner and foe alike? The entirety of the human race lives, succeeds, fails, learns, grows and dies on the same blue marble in this space-time matrix. Each and every soul on the planet is interconnected to each and every other soul by an invisible, unbreakable bond in this human experience, this quantum reality. Giving each and every one of us complete and total access to information sent and received by the other souls. Because of our quantum entanglement, the energy of your actions in Bangor, Maine is instantaneously transmitted faster than the speed of light to other souls in Tierra del Fuego, Beijing, Paris, Johannesburg and all points in between.

In 1997, Princeton psychologist, Roger Nelson, began a massive study called the Global Consciousness Project (GCP). Using a global network of computers, each running a random number generator (RNG) twenty-four hours a day, seven days a week, he studied the effects of the inner connection of group consciousness on highly emotional events around the globe like spiritual gatherings, famous weddings and deaths of celebrities.

More Than He Bargained For

To understand how the project works we have to put our gaming hats on. When people gamble certain energy is created. That energy has an effect on the game they are playing. That energy affects whether they win or lose. Gamblers talk about going on streaks. Winning streaks and losing streaks. I know people who always win at slot machines or poker. Our friend, Barb, was sitting next to us waiting to board a plane home from Las Vegas. She grew restless and said, "That machine's calling me." She jumped up and started playing slots. Barb won $300 in about ten minutes. When the streak was over she felt it and quit. She does that all the time. I've seldom known her to have a losing experience. Barb's gaming life, gambling and business, even Tupperware parties is one long winning streak. She is a Realtor, and I've also never seen her take on a client for whom she fails to find or sell a house. She's told me that when she meets a potential buyer she can tell by their energy whether they are going to buy from her or not.

The casinos know this energy is a very real thing. Another friend, Dave, is an extremely strong willed man. He owned the website I was working for when Penelope and I discovered Quantum Selling. Dave is a world-class code writer and very good at math. He won at blackjack in every casino we went to. He was my client and he wanted company. Well, one night while I was playing penny slots Dave was killing the blackjack table at the Golden Nugget. He was up several thousands and the casino had gone through three dealers trying the kill his winning energy. Dave knew what they were doing and he just shrugged it off and kept on winning. Then a frumpy looking guy in a cheap brown suit and frayed, polyester sports shirt joined Dave's table. Dave told me later he was sure the pit boss called him. The frumpy guy was a streak killer. He was a died-in-the-wool loser. His energy was so tuned to loss it was depressing to be around him. Dave lost a couple hands and cashed in his chips. He told me there was no cure for a streak killer. He kills your winning energy.

Basketball players talk about going into a shooting zone. When Kobe Bryant made 81 points against the Timberwolves to set the record for second most points in an NBA game after Wilt Chamberlain's 100, he simply could not miss. I personally watched him play that game. It was a thing of beauty. It didn't matter if he had a clear shot, or if he was falling over backward out of bounds. He put the ball in the hoop. He was in a zone. Football teams often talk about how they could feel the momentum carry them to victory. How they knew they would win before the game even started. Joe Namath guaranteed the upstart NY Jets would win Super Bowl III. He claims he knew they would win ahead of time. He could just "feel it." This energetic field that players talk about is also very real. In science, they would say this energetic field is a deviation from norm, or entropy. Because normally we would expect the game to be won by the better cards, the better team, the players with greater skill. The streak or zone is an aberration. It's not normal. It is unusual. It is not the even playing field we expect.

A Random Number Generator (RNG) is a computer program that electronically flips a coin over and over again, constantly. Twenty-four hours a day, seven days a week. It simulates the norm. The RNG reflects the norm of the energetic field we have come to expect from a coin toss. We expect the results of all this coin tossing to result in a fairly even split, 50 percent tails and 50 percent heads. Turns out, when a group of people experience heightened emotions, either happy or sad, they can alter the energetic field and create an entropy. The energetic field of the group consciousness affects the outcome of our coin toss. Instead of getting an even split of heads and tails we get a lop-sided result. Instead of a 50/50 split we get maybe a 10/90 split. We get a disturbance in the force, to borrow a Star Wars term. We get a deviation from the norm. We get an entropy and that we can measure.

This measurement tells us how any particular physical event affects the greater group consciousness. Since the RNG computers were running non-stop around the globe whenever something happened, we got a measurement.

Measurements of unusual disturbances in the force were expressed in terms of odds against chance. Or, what are the odds we could get this particular lopsided result by chance? Obviously, a 45/55 split is more possible than a 10/90 split. The televised funeral of Pope John Paul II, for example, shows a disturbance in our global consciousness, which begins at the start of the funeral and for a few hours rises in intensity, culminating with a high of odds against chance of 42 to 1. This entropy lasted for a few hours, and was centered primarily in Italy. Imagine a horse with those odds winning its two-minute race. If you bet on him, you'd have cleaned up, right? You'd win $42 for every $1 you bet. A two-dollar bet would pay you $84; a $100 bet would pay you $4,200. And if you bet $1,000, you would win $42,000. Now, that would be something to talk about. Obviously, that two-minute race would make quite an impact on you, right? You'd feel it, everyone in the stands would feel it and everyone watching Sports Center the next day would feel it. Powerful, right? Now, imagine every man woman and child in Italy being impacted as powerfully as you were, except the impact lasted for a few hours not two minutes. (Entropy makes no distinction between happy and sad. It is just a measurement of disturbance.) I'm sure you agree, we can say with certainty that The Pope's funeral had a powerful, sustained and measurable effect on people, especially in Italy.

The much-anticipated arrival of Y2K showed even stronger results. The media had hyped people worldwide for months that the arrival of the Year 2000 could cause major havoc among governments, businesses and banks, because of a programming glitch in their computers. People feared, among other things, that their life savings would be lost and that their lives would be turned upside down. This fear proved unfounded, but the disturbance in the worldwide consciousness was real, especially in the developed countries. It began a few minutes before midnight December 31, 1999, had a much shorter duration, but registered a high of odds against chance of 100 to 1. It was much more impactful on the global consciousness, but not as long lasting. You can read an expanded account of this and the following data in Dean Radin's book, *Entangled Minds*, mentioned in the previous chapter. I remember thinking how amazing it was to get an actual measurement of these disturbances. Now, the disturbance that happened on September 11, 2001 was a different story all together.

How Could They Know?

The disturbance in our human consciousness on that day began rising about 8 hours before the first plane crashed into the World Trade Center. Eight hours before it crashed! That means the hijackers probably hadn't even started getting dressed for the flight. The effect was registered fairly evenly across the globe. Eight hours before it happened!

What!

How could that be? How is it possible? How could people in Australia, the Pacific Rim, South America, North America, India, Europe, Africa and Asia – over seven billion souls – how could they all know this event was going to happen eight hours before it happened? How?

How could they know?

How did the knowledge of this event travel not only through all of humanity, but backwards in time? This information couldn't have been distributed to the world populace through a terrorist word-of-mouth campaign. There were only a handful of instigators who even knew about it and they wanted to keep their actions a secret. What if something foiled the attack and stopped the event from ever happening? The hijackers could have been discovered by security before they boarded the plane. They could have had a flat tire on the way to the airport and missed their flight entirely. A hundred things could have happened, but they didn't. The planes did complete their deadly mission. Their dramatic suicide attack and the impact it created were unprecedented, completely unpredictable. A foreign aggressor has not successfully attacked the continental USA since the War of 1812. No, the information could only have been sent after the event occurred. Only after those two planes crashed into the World Trade Center killing so many and causing so much horror and chaos. Billions of human beings worldwide knew. They reacted dramatically to an unexpected and unpredictable event that happened eight hours in the future. Most of those people have absolutely zero understanding of entropy, quantum entanglement or time travel. Or much less do they care. No, these are ordinary, everyday human beings without 23rd Century super powers of any kind. Yet they experienced a precognitive presentiment of this event a full eight hours before the crash took place.

Take a moment and process the power of this information.

Do you remember what you experienced September 11, 2001? A friend called and woke Diane and me. Diane was recovering from emergency surgery, so we were sleeping in. A friend called and said, "Turn on the TV. Any channel." The screen came alive as the second plane flew deliberately into the second tower, confirming it was not a horrible accident. We couldn't even talk for several minutes. Apparently, neither could the reporter because nobody said anything. We just watched as the plane became a gigantic fireball and the building full of people fell in a nightmare of black smoke. There was no doubt the United States of America was under attack. The richest, most secure nation on earth, protected by the largest and most powerful military force in the world has ever known had just suffered a crushing blow. And the first causality was the financial center in New York City. Do you remember your experience? I'll never forget mine. Did you experience the energy of undeniable dread? Well, people all over the world experienced that energy. Unconsciously, seven billion souls experienced that energy eight full hours before it ever happened!

The disturbance in the force experienced for 9/11 was significantly higher than the other two. Whereas Pope John Paul II's funeral registered odds against chance of 42 to 1 and Y2K registered odds against chance of 100 to 1 the attack on New York City, September 11, 2001, blew the top off the charts. That attack was so impacting on so many human beings it registered odds against chance of 1,000,000 to 1. Worldwide. **A million to one!** Who would like to collect on a horse with those odds? That would be a return of $2,000,000 on a $2 investment. This one event impacted the global consciousness to an alarming degree never seen before or since. It makes you rethink everything you ever thought you knew about how the world works, doesn't it? It tells us one thing for sure.

Information absolutely can be sent backward in time. Einstein was proven right! There is no such thing as a time barrier.

The only thing preventing you and me from sending messages to a different physical place and into a different time frame in our space-time continuum is our willingness to do it. It's as easy and doable as swiping your new smart phone calendar backwards to see when you had your last haircut.

When you do go to sleep tonight do so knowing absolutely, positively, beyond all doubt, without even the slightest possibility of error that you can send a Miracle Healing to me back in the early morning hours of March 29, 2009. Which I sincerely hope you do, because your willingness to send it confirms your acceptance of infinite possibility as an actionable reality. The act of sending that message to me in the Presence of the Generous One activates the power of your Miracle Healing. Your willingness to send a healing message back to me in the past, and into another dimension of reality anoints your healing message with a unique and powerful blessing. It guarantees your Miracle Healing will be sanctioned by the Ultimate Power of All-Creation, because it already has been. Your action gives your Miracle Healing the Divine Power to deliver unprecedented healing and infinite abundance.

This is the gift you asked me to bring back for you. This is the Gift, which gave me a second life and allowed me a full and complete recovery. This is the Gift of Miracle Healing you created in the Presence of the Generous One.

This is the Gift for which you've been waiting.

Thank you for your life-giving gift. Thank you for joining us. We few, we powerful few, who are living a life of unabridged consciousness and making such a difference in the world, thank you for helping to heal our precious transformational playground.

The delivery of this message acknowledges your acceptance of the infinite possibility of abundance as an actionable reality. It is my deliverance and the deliverance of all you love.

This is your deliverance.

All Healing
Begins With
A Desire
To Heal

CHAPTER 17
A Miracle Moment

The very first thing I must tell you is also the last thing I must tell you – you may have picked this up by now.

You can do this.

I know you can do this. Because you did it before. Good grief, you did it again just a few chapters ago. I was there both times. I watched you create a Miracle Healing. I received the healing message you sent. I am a living testament to the fact it was a full-blown, life-giving, life-changing divine miracle. I am alive, walking, talking, writing and, thank the stars above, watching television because of the Miracle Healing you created. I am enjoying a full and complete recovery because of the Miracle Healing you created in the Presence of the Generous One.

After my massive stroke in the emergency room and I was resting uncomfortably in ICU, Penelope went home and sent out an email request to about 50,000 of our closest friends, asking them to send me a healing. And thank God they did send their healing. These blessed folks sent it because I needed it, desperately. They used the healing protocols with which they were familiar. They sent prayers. They went into the Portal. They acted out of love and sent healing thoughts. Without thinking about quantum field theory, the existence of an afterlife or the feasibility of time travel. They simply sent me a healing from their hearts. That was my first rainbow of Miracle Healing. At least, I thought it was.

I am eternally grateful.

Oh, by the way, you were part of that group. When you sent your first healing message a few chapters back it was right after I recounted my first death experience. That was when Penelope sent her email. Oh, I know sometimes all this space-time quantum-reality stuff sounds like mumbo-jumbo, but you would be shocked to your core if you knew the veracity and relevance of the connections we easily dismiss as mere coincidence. The fact remains your healing message joined with all those folks responding to Penelope's email back in 2009 because it was sent from love and it was your first.

I told you that your timing was great.

The healing energy of the two rainbows of Miracle Healing was equally important to my immediate well being as well as my full and complete recovery. Differentiating between the two is a fool's errand. The important thing to remember is you have already breathed life into my weary and battered soul. And you will do it again and again for a long time to come.

I know you will send it again and again for several reasons.

First of all you and I are one. We are the same. There is no difference between the two of us. Oh, we have some insignificant characteristics, preferences and appeal, but we share the same energy. To think otherwise would be a delusion of consciousness, right? Ok, you might choose a lobster dinner while I might choose prime rib or maybe a vegan salad, but that doesn't count for much, now does it? If you were in trouble and you asked me to send you a healing message back in time and into another dimension, I would do it, immediately. Especially, since it only takes a moment and I've already done it once anyway. Besides, sending the message showers love and joy on me. It feels fantastic! Man, I'd be a fool to refuse such a win/win investment. I invest a moment and get back love and joy. Wow, sign me up.

See this is probably the biggest reason you send that message again and again. You'll fall in love with the feedback. It's addicting. I send you a Miracle Healing many, many times every day. I send one when I get up in the morning. I send a couple in the shower. I always send one before I go into the Portal. I send one after I come out of the Portal. I send one at breakfast, lunch and dinner. While I watch the Lakers games. Before I go to bed. I love sending you and everyone else in the world a Miracle Healing. *It only takes a moment.* Anytime I know of someone who is sick or in desperate need I send them a Miracle Healing. When I drive by a homeless person I send a Miracle Healing. When Diane forces me to watch the news I send one about every five minutes. Especially when someone does something I find absolutely deplorable, I send them a Miracle Healing.

Oh, you'll love this. I always send someone a Miracle Healing when I'm feeling down or challenged in some way. Because it makes me stronger, healthier and so much more abundant. Because I know I'm helping someone else. Because the feedback from sending that Miracle Healing makes me feel great!

Keep in mind that we are one. *Mi energia es tu energia.* Your background, your education and your income don't matter. Your age, your color, your language doesn't matter. Your beliefs, your politics and religion don't matter because we share the same energy. We are different versions of each other. We are mirror images of each other. If you hurt, I hurt. If you are causing others pain then I am causing others pain. *Mi energia es tu energia.* Consequently, if you are showered with healing, love and joy, I am showered with healing, love and joy. We both breathe the same air, swim in the same waters and walk on the same blue marble in this amazing space-time continuum. If I send you a Miracle Healing, then I'm also sending me a Miracle Healing.

Words Words Words

What you say is not as important as your intention to send a healing message back to Tom Pauley in the early morning hours of March 29, 2009 into the Presence of the Generous One. That can be easily accomplished by picturing that Rainbow of Miracle Healing I received. The first or second is irrelevant. I always see that rainbow of Miracle Healing colors as a tight close up. There was no arch in it. It was simply alive with strong vibrant colors. Every color imaginable and then some.

Many religions have one or more healing prayers and chants. Use one of those, particularly if you have a favorite. The metaphysical community offers an excellent selection of healings and blessings. Ho'oponopono is a short and extremely effective secular option. My friend Dr. Joe Vitale made this popular in a couple of his many books. Or you can make up your own message. The words are not as important as actually taking action.

Here's my personal favorite:

Heal! Heal! Heal!

I like it because it short and powerful. *It only takes a moment.*

I got that command from Jack Houck at P.K. Party (spoon bending) in Anaheim, CA around the turn of the century. Jack was showing about fifty of us how to use quantum energy to sprout seeds and bend spoons, forks and metal bars. I told two stainless steel spoons in my hands to bend and they melted like butter. I have never looked at life the same again after that. I gathered the quantum energy with my mind. I spoke to my spoons with a loud, clear and forceful voice demanding that my spoons *Bend! Bend! Bend!* With my eyes closed and my focus on the spoons I sent the quantum energy surging down my head, neck and arms, then up through my hands and fingers into the spoons. It was beyond electric. Then, and this is the secret to making this process work, I detached completely. I had to let the quantum energy do the work. Once I had asked them to bend I had to let go of my desire. Not care about the outcome. Like I said, my spoons melted like butter.

I get highly energized just thinking about this.

After the party was over I talked to Jack. He told me one man became so proficient at calling quantum energy he did it unconsciously. The guy would walk through a local restaurant and the flat wear set on the tables he passed would curl up and bend in on themselves. He also said that a chiropractor friend used this procedure in his healing work with miraculous results.

Instead of saying: *Bend! Bend! Bend!*

The doctor said: *Heal! Heal! Heal!*

I took the idea for my healing work. It's shocking how well this works. In my mind I see energy building above me like an aurora in a rainbow of colors shifting and moving with fluid grace and ease, yet backed with the power and energy of the cosmos. I then demand that energy transport my healing message. I think of that Rainbow of Miracle Healing I received and with forceful intent say, aloud or silently: *Heal! Heal! Heal!* I can feel the healing message surging from my mind and then blast off to do its work.

Then I detach so it *can* do its work. I don't think about it again. Because I know Miracle Healing is delivered.

It only takes a moment.

Of course we need all the healing we can get, so I send more later. Needless to say, this is what I use personally when I send you a healing message back into the past and into the Presence of the Generous One to create a Miracle Healing for you.

I'll use this one in my directions, but as always you get to choose what is right for you.

The most important part is to keep where, when and to whom you are sending your healing message in your mind. You can picture a friend or foe to whom you wish to send a Miracle Healing. You already know Tom's story. You know where the powerful and blessed healing rainbow is. I've mentioned the time and place often enough. Holding the image of that Rainbow of Miracle Healing, send your healing message. It has already been consecrated as a Miracle Healing.

Since you are ready please follow these seven simple steps:

1. Close your eyes and think of all you wish to heal.
2. Hold a mental image of Tom infused by the Rainbow of Miracle Healing in the Presence of the Generous One.
3. Let the healing build strength, as the colors grow more and more vibrant.
4. Now, send your healing message in a blast of energy from your mind into the past.
5. Say: *Heal! Heal! Heal!*
6. Detach yourself completely from the outcome.

7. Embrace and savor the rebound of the Miracle Healing you created.

Repeat this exercise several times today. It will become almost an unconscious response after a while. Instead of using hand signals for a bad driver or a harsh words for a heartless act, send a Miracle Healing.

What an amazing power of change you wield!

Not everyone will accept your healing directly, but energy is never wasted. Good spreads. Every time you do it, be sure to detach and then stay open to receive the energy coming back to you. *Only takes a moment.*

CHAPTER 18
Safe And Protected

For many years I have counseled people to surrender their lives to God. To turn all their affairs over to their Higher Power. That they were not responsible for their successes or their failures. To leave their successes, their failures and their difficulties in the care of the Source of All-Creation. I told everyone not to worry about the changes and chances of the world because they were safe and protected at all times and under all conditions.

Once I had to live with my stroke, I began to seriously question the whole concept. I certainly wasn't safe from a massive stoke. After a few years I came to accept that I was never going to be physically the same as I was before the stroke.

I had begun to doubt. In the back of my mind one question ate at me. Why hadn't God kept me safe and protected from the horror of a stroke? Had I done something wrong? Or was that only an empty promise?

Oh, I clung to the full and complete recovery part because it was the only thing keeping me from giving up completely. Keeping me from rejecting everything I had come to believe about how the world works. Keeping me from disavowing the truth of everything I knew from my personal experience.

Trouble was, a seed of doubt was growing inside me. I questioned my connection to the All-Powerful Source of Truth. If He wasn't keeping me safe from a massive stroke, then I couldn't trust anything I had been given as truth. That meant I was lying. My job as a salesman was to honestly represent whatever I'm selling. I cannot sell a lie. I had lost my alignment with the Ultimate Source of my good.

I worked my business as best I could the first years of my recovery, but I wasn't moving ahead. I was only treading water. I didn't seem to have the same mojo I had before. I certainly lacked the old enthusiasm. What was missing? What did I need to do to get back to my work? The work I loved. I believed that work is worship. What was keeping me from my worship?

Maybe it was the economy. Were the mundane forces of the Great Recession working against me? Had business changed so much there was no way I'd ever catch up? Was I destined for the dust heap of those who tried and failed?

Maybe it was the stroke. Was I no longer physically or mentally capable of competing in the market place? Was I one of those who were blown overboard by the storms of outrageous fortune and swept away by the seas of despair and lost hope? All I needed was a little direction. Just an inkling of guidance.

Instead I was given a torment. More and more everyday I'd wake up thinking about writing this book, which I quickly dismissed as an exercise in pretense, or heaven forbid, hubris. At least, that is what I told myself. I was an ordinary human, a human who doubted. How could I be chosen to write about a deeper and more relevant understanding of the human experience? I needed to right my business and continue to bring good folks everywhere the basics of how you can take control of your life, leave poverty behind and live the life you came into this world to live as I had once done. Besides, I wouldn't even know how to begin or what to write about. I knew the Angel Gabriel choked Mohammed until He allowed Himself to receive Divine Guidance. But I am not a Manifestation of God. I am just a man.

What I didn't want to accept was that the real hubris is thinking you can do anything other than that which the Generous One gives you to do."

When you deviate from your path. When you avoid the test or challenge on your path. When you refuse to do what your higher power has given you to do. Then you are given other difficulties, other choices with harder consequences designed to turn you around, get you back on your correct path.

Diane and I have a dear friend, Jillian Coleman Wheeler, whom we have known for more years than any of us wants me to mention. Well, maybe Diane. She doesn't seem to get the concept of secrets. Jillian and we have helped one another through so many difficulties in each other's lives.

Jillian delights in quoting me back to me when the shoe fits. I was bemoaning my predicament to her one day. After a brief pause she said, "Don't you remember that story you told in the Rich Dreams book? About the man who dies in a flood not because God wanted him to die. But because the man refused to get into one of the two boats or the helicopter God sent to rescue him? That's you right now, Tom. Get in the boat. Write the book!"

"But I don't know what to write. Don't know the through line. I don't know anything about it. I'm flying blind here.

Besides how do I even know what I get is true."

"Oh come on. You blew through how many careers, forty something, right? Every time you felt like your life was over and that you were bound to live the rest of your life in poverty and humiliation, you would find a way to start over and you'd end up better than ever."

"Yeah, but this is different...."

"Stop! You didn't have a through line when you sold most of your earthly possessions and moved the whole family to New Mexico for your faith or to California to write movies. You just did it. What did you tell me, 'you are loved and protected at all times and under all conditions?' So write the book already!"

Loved and Protected! Of course, if you are loved by God you are safe. And you are always safe in God's love. The words are interchangeable here. As Dave Edman would say, "Insight is a wonderful thing."

Writing the book was the direction I was waiting for. It was in front of me all the time. Often the guidance and direction you desperately desire are presenting themselves to you every day. But you ignore them because they don't fit into your own predefined notion of what they should be. All too often you are suffering from this problem or that and you see the solution as more money, another job, more business, a better drug, or new love when that's not even close to what you need. I didn't need to right my business, the business God gave me in the first place. No, what I needed was to write the book and in the process gain the healing I'd come to the earthly experience to have.

So I started writing, knowing that I am safe/loved and protected at all times and under all conditions.

Still, I didn't understand exactly why things were going wrong in my life. There's no reason why I had to lose so much while I followed my path. Apparently, I needed more healing.

I was writing, but I was struggling financially, once again. No matter how much came in, it wasn't enough. Money was flowing out faster than floodwaters over a busted dam. I should have recognized the sign. I should have started acting on the direction I had received and found my alignment, but alas, my ego knew better.

I had grown completely frustrated by my constantly reduced living standard. Never mind I lived in a large, beautiful house in a resort community. A home that was the gathering place of all family events because no one else had one nearly as big. No, I decided I had to have it out with God for His inattention to my very important needs. Before our dinner guests arrived one Saturday night I went out back on the portico to the trusty camp chair I used for going into the Portal. I was primed to get this low-income nonsense straightened out once and for all. As I bent over, but before I could get my backside in that chair I heard a very loud, powerful voice in my head say:

"Do you have a bed to sleep in? Do you have a roof over your head? Do you have food to eat and friends to share it with? You have one job, Tom. Writing the book. That's your job. We'll take care of everything else. You are safe and protected at all times and under all conditions."

Now you would think that message would certainly be convincing enough to keep me focused. It was an impossible-to-ignore, an otherworldly message spoken directly to me. Not many folks get that kind of direction. The message was clear enough. Tom writes the book and a power far greater than anyone can possibly imagine takes care of everything else.

Simple, right?

Well, maybe not if your ego was wound as tight as mine was. I tried to relax and release control for a few months. Of course at the same time I failed to focus completely on my assignment. I sat down every day, but what came out was not ready for prime time. It was more an exercise in obfuscation. My ego didn't want to give up control.

I just couldn't let go. Giving up control of your life is really difficult. Trusting in the Source of All Creation is trying when faced with apparent mortal loss, failure and humiliation. Especially if you're a bull-headed, get 'er done kind of guy who always thinks he knows better about everything.

About eight months after that verbal warning which should have put my fears to rest, I was coming home in my Jeep from a day of freeway driving culminating with a fifty-dollar haircut in Huntington Beach. All day I had been struggling with the concept of my protection. I had been assured I had one job and one job only. Write the book! Not right my income. Write the book. I was guided to write this book and They would take care of everything else. I was still not completely satisfied with the job They were doing. Never mind that I was not making any progress on the book!

The only reality I could see was one in which there wasn't enough money. I had some big expenses. Consequently, I would periodically complain. That day I was driving across Orange County doing errands while mentally throwing up a constant stream of complaints in my thoughts. Demanding answers I'd already been given. Well, I got another answer. I didn't like the answer, but it was exactly the answer I needed. Something I wouldn't forget.

I was coming home on the 405 freeway, my thoughts fixed on my business and financial difficulties. I started pulling across the five lanes heading south. It was late in the afternoon and traffic was getting heavy. I was going seventy-five, when I heard a loud bang, like I'd hit a large piece of metal in the road which flew up and smashed into my oil pan. The car shook from the apparent collision. It really startled me. I watched for an oil light. Nothing came on. I debated stopping, but at the time I was busy maneuvering through the steady stream of cars to my exit, the 133 highway to Laguna Beach. About a mile from the freeway there's a stoplight on the 133. I could see the flashing yellow lights warning me I'd have to stop as I rounded the turn off, so I took my foot off the gas. That might have saved my life.

As I slowed for a stoplight on the 133 I heard another much louder BANG! Accompanied by the crunching and grinding sounds of metal ripping apart, the death throes of a shattered and frozen transmission. The tires immediately stopped turning. I skidded and bounced to a jarring stop. The car would not move another inch nor would it go into neutral. The transmission was a goner, dead and locked tight. In a matter of seconds, I had become a sitting target on a major six-lane highway during evening rush hour. I was not confident in limping across the busy four-lane highway in sixty-five mph traffic without the benefit of a crosswalk. My insides were still shaking from the frightening transmission failure. Do I risk my life by hobbling across the highway with my stroke-weakened body or do I wait until someone smashes into my car at full speed while their attention is elsewhere? People aren't necessarily thinking about the road after a long day at work. Thank God, the ever-abiding Source of all Creation loved and protected me, once again. Before the light changed to green, a young woman police officer in a Ford 350 pickup pulled behind my severely wounded Jeep Liberty, protecting my flank. Then, as if summoned by the Concourse on High, eight motorcycle cops on their way to a rally surrounded my vehicle, further protecting me. I told the sergeant what happened. He looked at me and shaking his head said, "Man, if that transmission had frozen up seconds earlier, you'd be toast right now. You are one lucky man."

Lucky? Or was I safe and protected at all times and under all conditions?

Now I shouldn't have needed more proof. I should have persevered. Trusted that I was protected. Surrendered my life to the Supreme Force of All-Creation. I had been given a lifetime of proof. Writing this book was my path. I thought I knew better.

The ego never wants to surrender.

Patience and perseverance can be difficult lessons to learn even under the best of conditions. These days are not the best of conditions, my friends. Conditions in the world are growing worse by the minute. Check out the evening news. Compared to a year earlier it's exponentially worse. We do not have time to waste. It would be nice if we could digest this information slowly and try it out little by little. It would be nice to have the slow pace of yesterday.

We do not have the time for slow learning. We need to embrace the maturation our experiences have given us. This is the time for knowing. Knowing that our purpose is to grow and expand. Knowing that making money alone is not our purpose. Money is only the means that can help us fulfill our purpose. Knowing that as long as we fulfill our purpose everything else will be taken care of. Knowing we can still have the rich abundant life we seek without giving up our integrity, our time or all we love. It is the time for knowing that we are loved and protected at all times and under all conditions.

This is the time for action.

Time Is Of The Essence

Yes, I was protected, but that didn't mean I was excused from my work. Instead of seeking alignment with the Lord of all-Creation for the tests given me, I followed the guidance of my ego. The day I nearly turned into toast on the 405 freeway and nearly died on the 133, I had spent the whole day grumbling to the One who covers all knowledge about my difficult situation. Demanding to know why I am required to endure such difficulties.

Truth is, life is not all about me. Nor is it all about you. We both have a bigger job to do than making ourselves comfortable. Our job is to first connect and align with the Source of all that is and then follow our path.

How unbearably arrogant I was! I had been given wonderful gifts, talents and abilities. My path had led me to an incredible understanding and training which prepared me for the most honorable and venerated mission of bringing you this gift of Miracle Healing. I had been given a direct connection to guides and angels to help dispel my fears and keep me on track. I have been given not one, but two audiences in the Presence of the Generous One. I have been given a second chance to get things right. Still, I doubted! I dared to question the Generous One.

Who was I to question Source? Thankfully, all I got for my arrogance was a more forceful lesson. A wake-up call. It could have been much worse.

Marilyn loved reminding us that when you fail to do your work, first you lose your money, then your health, then your life.

I know I may sound like someone who doesn't appreciate all he has, but then who does? We, each and every one, are unappreciative of the glorious richness of our lives or the impossibly vast array of opportunities available to us. When difficulty pops its trying head into our path, we tend to think back on our own strengths and weaknesses, back on our past tests and look for solutions. We think about what we once did to solve a problem. We think of the past as a guide to the tests we face today. This is not the answer.

Relying strictly on your own ego-driven choices can have you speeding toward a fiery crash. Staying open and connecting to divine guidance is paramount for your success.

Follow Your Path

I have a neighbor, Mark. I think of him as the brother I never had. He was a wealthy doctor, who because of his choices lived on the street in Laguna Beach for a number of years. One of the homeless we try not to see. He was not following his path as a healer. He was off course. There was nothing he could possibly do to make that life a success. He was being told every day to turn around and go back, as painful and difficult as that must have seemed. He'd lost everything he ever had. He'd lost all his money and all his things. He'd lost his license to practice. He'd lost his wife and son. He'd even lost his left eye. He had nothing left, but himself. His wounded, dying self. His future must have seemed hopeless, impossibly hopeless. Finally his tests became so severe that he gave up. He stopped making decisions spawned by his flawed human ego. He followed the divine guidance we all receive every minute of our lives once we silence the ego noise and listen. He found healing by aligning with his Higher Power, the All-Abiding Power of Creation.

My friend faced his pain and allowed himself to be guided back to his given path. Trusting that he was loved and protected at all times and under all conditions. Now he lives in a beautiful home in a gated community with sculptured lawns and 553 varieties of trees, an 18 hole championship golf course, a 9 hole par three course, eight club houses, one devoted entirely to bridge, seven swimming pools and an equestrian center. I'm reading from the brochure. He owns a beautiful dressage gelding, which he keeps at an even more up-scale stable for training. Mark has come a long way from his low point. Today he runs a chiropractic publishing company while he guides and coaches those who have lost their way as he did. Once again he's doctoring the sick and wounded and living in comfort. He told me recently that he is happier and more satisfied with his life than he has ever been. My friend didn't really lose a single thing he cared about, except his wife and son, of course. Oh, I know he'd love to have the eye back, but as hard as it seems, this world has real choices with real consequences. Mark would be the first to tell you how good life can be when you turn your life over to the Source of all your good.

Mark became a quantum magnet for the rewarding and successful life he desires because he found alignment with his Higher Power. This is the secret to Infinite Abundance.

Regardless of what you think you have lost or might lose. Regardless of how bad you might think your life has become. Regardless of how difficult you might believe the road ahead is, you can still enjoy the wealth of abundance you came here to enjoy. Face your pain, watch for the signs of change and above all follow your path.

I am healing centuries of hidden pain. Which when you think about it, is exactly what these tests are intended to do. I have been forced to stretch and expand my consciousness and widen my perspective. I am becoming a more whole and complete version of me. Sure, I sometimes bemoan my plight, but then who doesn't? We're only human. I must remind myself all the time that life is not meant to be one day of ease followed by another day of ease. Where's the growth in that? We cannot redo the same tests we faced before. We're past them. We've done them. Our new tests must challenge our deepest understanding of who we think we are, inspiring us to become all we can become. In the end I am eternally grateful for every trying moment. Because every time I complete a test, every time I make a choice and deal with the consequences, I stand a little taller, grow a whole lot wiser and become infinitely richer.

Any of this sound familiar? Are you following your path, regardless of where it leads? Are you facing your pain, regardless of where that leads? Are you eschewing the call of your ego and staying in alignment with the All Knowing Source of all that is?

I am enjoying a full and complete recovery. I am healing every aspect of who I am. You can, too. You can heal your own centuries of hidden pain. You can become whole again. You can become a powerful quantum magnet attracting healing and success into your life faster than the speed of light.

Our precious transformational playground needs your help. Humanity is desperately ill. If you doubt that, simply look around you. The signs are everywhere. People are deeply divided by religion, politics, race, culture, education, affluence, appearance, and personal desires – every artificial measure we construct to explain our separateness. Terror and violence are commonplace. Unusually severe and devastating weather has become routine. Waste and destruction of the planet fueled by greed and avarice is praised. Anger and hate are elevated to the level of righteousness. *The fire of separation is consuming us all.* We are not separate from one another. We are one another. Your friends, your family and your despised enemies are all part of you. The earth, the weather and the stars are not separate from you. They are you. They are all part of you. Everything in your life is part of you, which means you are in great need of healing. The only way to heal you is to heal them.

To think otherwise is a delusion of consciousness.

Where will this perilous ego-fueled sickness of separateness lead? Is this the future you want? Is this the good you seek for yourself? For those you love? Of course not. No sane person would. This is not the road to Infinite Abundance. This is not happiness and success.

You have it in your power to do something about the direction you take and by so doing, calm the chaos and magnify the beacon of peace for all of us. Your healing message can help stop the wanton destruction of our transformational playground. You can heal them. You have already created a Miracle Healing.

You can do it again.

All those you love need you. Only you can do what you do. Your children can't do what you do. Nor can Microsoft, Berkshire-Hathaway, Bank of America, or any of the Fortune 500 do what you do. All the governments and armies of the world can't do what you do. Even if they could somehow join together and assist one another they cannot do what you do. Nobody can. You have amazing and totally unique powers. Powers you didn't even know you had. Powers you activate by your willingness to love and heal. No one else can do the things you do.

You are the one.

You cannot do everything by yourself, of course. And you certainly cannot do what you were never meant to do. You can only follow your path. Do your part so others can do theirs. Maybe your part is raising the next generation, making key decisions for a multi-national corporation, working on an assembly line, standing a post in a foreign land, writing a book or a song, making dinner for your family, encouraging a friend who is down, educating a few or entertaining millions. No job is too small or too big. Whatever your path calls for you to do – just do it.

All you can do is what your path leads you to do. Rest assured, you do your part brilliantly and it is absolutely necessary. You need help, of course. Creating a world where peace, love and endless abundance can thrive is no small feat. No one can do it alone. Follow your path and send your Miracle Healing every single day of your life.

This is the brilliantly colored orb of healing you held high to calm the storm in my living video. This is the life-giving gift I brought back especially for you. This is the Miracle Healing that saved my life. Send it again and often. It holds divine power. This is how you do your part. Not by extraordinary effort. Not by doing what you were never meant to do. Send your Miracle Healing daily and the storms begin to quiet. *Only takes a moment.* Your Miracle Healing spreads throughout humankind by the same quantum connection that spread the energy of 9/11. Only this time the energy was healing energy. Silently. Universally. Powerfully. All that you love is healed. Our transformational playground is healed. All this happens organically because you helped someone else heal with no thought for yourself.

I know for a fact you do your part well. Because I saw you do it. What a thrill it is to watch you. Nothing can stop you. Nothing. You are magnificent, impervious to the storms of scarcity consciousness, which surge against you, threatening to destroy all hope of goodness and abundance. Your strength, your courage and your steadfastness are the stuff of legend.

Becoming
A Magnet
For Infinite
Abundance

CHAPTER 19
Calling The Arc

It has always been a challenge for humans to grasp the duplicity of our space-time matrix. Let alone fully comprehend how to function within its dual nature. When I need help, I call the Arc of Light. When I am confused and unsure what to do, I call the Arc of Light. When I am afraid, worried and feel like I have no resources available to me, I call the Arc of Light. There I find comfort, reassurance and guidance. There I feel safe and protected from the slings and arrows of life's more daunting challenges. There I can connect to energy and guidance of a transcendent power.

For many years I have sought to stay in alignment with God, but I would inevitably become distracted. I would, for example, align more with abundance than with the Source of all abundance. It was important that I align with abundance so I could function and thrive in this world. That, however, could not become my only or even my foremost point of alignment. It skewed my thinking and my decision-making. Aligning with the Arc of Light keeps me on my path. It gives me the solace and comfort I need when I need it. Aligning with the Arc of Light has given me a peace I didn't have before.

When I was in the Arc of Light in the Presence of the Generous One during my second death experience, I received two separate waves of Miracle Healing. I mentioned this earlier. Twice a torrent of rainbow healing flooded my essence. I want to try and give you an idea of what it felt like.

I was in a state of complete peace in the perfectly serene beauty and bounty of the Arc. Seeing all I needed to see. Hearing all I needed to hear to make a dispassionate decision whether to go on to the next world or go back to my earthly experience. I have never known nor could have known the total peace I felt at that moment. Nothing could touch me. Nothing could threaten me. Nothing could harm me. I was in a state of peace and calm beyond all understanding. The instant I decided I would return, the first magnificent Miracle Healing rainbow burst through the Living Light and assaulted my essence. The sheer force of it hit my chest and knocked me backward. I know I didn't have a body, but that's how it felt. I keep saying it was dimmer than the second, but at that moment I considered the first rainbow was the most brilliant thing I'd ever known.

Quicker than I could comprehend what had happened, the second rainbow of Miracle Healing exploded through the walls of the Arc of Light. The reason I saw this force as coming through a wall is that I was in the Presence of the Generous One. I was in a chamber, a place sanctified above and beyond all that is. I also realized that this rainbow of love and healing energy originated somewhere else. This gargantuan force of healing energy – greater in size, shape, and intensity of color blasted through my heart and blew my insides completely out. Impossible, I know. I didn't have any inside or outside, let alone heart. This is amazingly difficult to explain. That second rainbow was so powerful and assaulted my being with such force that for one sublime moment I lost all sense of my own existence.

That Miracle Healing rainbow cleansed me inside out. It blew all that was unnecessary and abhorrent completely out of my being. In fact, for one unforgettable moment nothing existed for me except that glorious healing rainbow. I know that seems like a contradiction to the fact that I was one with the Generous One at the time. I can't explain any of it properly. Best I can do is share a feeling of what it was like. Those two rainbows of Miracle Healing were so impacting on me that they are indelibly etched in my mind. Still today it is those loving incredibly brilliant, real yet supernaturally beautiful rainbows of Miracle Healing that I remember from my second death experience.

When I visualize that second Miracle Healing Rainbow I still feel the impact of it assaulting my heart and penetrating my being with pure sweet divine love. A deep intense love. A love that can move mountains into the sea. This is only the beginning of what your healing message can do once it is transmuted into a Miracle Healing in the Presence of the Generous One. Imagine the effect on everything and everyone you love once it is expanded, multiplied and returned to you.

I've been avoiding using the word assault in reference to a Miracle Healing, but that's exactly what it was. I have been hearing the word every time I remembered that Miracle Healing Rainbow, but I hesitated saying anything because I thought I was protecting you from the word assault. Truth is you must know the awful and transforming power of your own Miracle Healing. The Miracle Healing you created was an overwhelmingly awesome assault on all that is abhorrent and contrary to a healthy, peaceful and loving existence.

Scarcity consciousness cannot be eradicated with a summer breeze. We need the same force of God that knocked Saul of Tarsus to the ground and blinded him for three days. We need the same overwhelmingly powerful force that turned Lot's wife into a pillar of salt and raised Lazarus from the dead. Your Miracle Healing carries every bit of that force and more.

I don't know if you will ever fully recognize what a fabulous gift you created. I don't know if you can because its power emanates from the Infinite, the Source of All Creation. I am of course indebted to you for my life and my continued healing. You sent me a healing message backwards in time and into another dimension creating a Miracle Healing in the Presence of the Generous One. Your action gave me life. It allowed me to bring this brilliantly colored orb of comprehension, this book of understanding, this opportunity for Miracle Healing energy back for you to hold in your heart, which you will naturally and effortlessly pass to others. What an amazingly kind, generous and virtuous thing you've done.

Deepening Your Healing Message

Now, I'm going to show you how to deepen your healing message. The more you understand, the more you allow yourself to see, the more elevated your consciousness becomes, the more powerful your healing message will be.

It, too, takes only a moment.

This simple action of sending a Miracle Healing is invigorating and very compelling. Here's how you can elevate and enhance the impact of your message.

We are going to start by calling the energy of the Arc of Light into your earthly experience. This is another image, which will empower your visualizations. Actually, the Arc does not come to you. You align with the Arc. You, however, will picture that alignment as the Arc coming to you. Now the act of aligning with something as divinely powerful and void of any physical world reference as the Arc of Light can be a little tricky. For years Those Voices I hear would tell me I was out of alignment and I needed to get back in alignment, but for the life of me I didn't know how to do that. I didn't know what actions to take to accomplish that task. The steps listed below are how you can visualize and align to the Arc of Light so you can send Tom a healing message in the Presence of the Generous One. This will automatically connect you with your Transcendent Self because only unity is possible in the Arc. Separation is absurd. You are forever connected with Tom, the Generous One and all that is. This is a great exercise for connection and aligning with the All-Encompassing Power of Creation.

You create a Miracle Healing. You heal Tom so he can bring this book back. You heal all that you love in this life. You connect to Source. You do all this with your eyes closed in only a few moments.

Do this exercise:

Go into a quiet safe place. Turn off all possible sources of distraction, including phones and computers of all kinds. What you are about to do is one of the most important actions you can possibly take. Once you become familiar with finding this connection you will be able to do it on a busy subway, in the middle of a joyous celebration or taking off in a jet airplane, but for now limit the distractions.

Close your eyes and imagine walking through a forest on a cloudless and moonless night. Look up at the billions of trillions of stars in our known universe and allow that visualization of infinity surround you. Allow your essence to ascend into the beautiful and womb-like darkness of the beginning that has no ending. Hold a pure loving intention. You are motivated only by a desire to do good for someone else. In your mind call the energy of the Arc of Light to come to you. A point of living, All-Knowing Light descends, growing larger as it does. Let the omnipotent Arc of Light surround you, superseding all other existence. Allow yourself to merge completely with this loving, healing Light. Allow your earthly fears and concerns to vanish into the brilliance of the Light.

Imagine Tom's body lying in a bed in the ICU at Saddleback Hospital in Laguna Hills, California on March 29, 2009. Your intention is to heal this earthly manifestation of Tom Pauley. That will send your healing message back in time-space. Not because you hope to gain, nor save the world, but because Tom needs your help.

Now focus your mind on the rainbow of Miracle Healing that assaulted Tom and send your healing message into the Presence of the Generous One.

The Generous One has already invested your healing message with the power of a Miracle Healing.

Now, this is important!
Allow your mind to gather the force of a Class 5 hurricane. You've seen satellite views, picture one now in your mind in your favorite color or better yet in a rainbow of colors. This is your healing. Let it build in strength and power. You will see, feel or simply know when your healing has gathered enough strength. I see the colors grow more vibrant. That's how I

know. When you've built enough strength in your healing blast your healing from your mind with great force and say the words:

Heal! Heal! Heal!

It's more emphatic to say the words out loud if you can. You are commanding your healing message, not begging it. Tell it you mean business. You want healing now! If you need to say them in your mind, do it with the same commanding intent.

Picture your healing gift exploding forth in a rainbow of colors, aromas, fragrances and textures as your healing message joins the healing energy sent by others and is transformed instantly into a Miracle Healing. Accompanied by the most inspiring and enlightening music in creation. The color and frequency of your Miracle Healing is a wonder to taste, so refreshing, clean and uncompromising. The melody is uplifting and enlightening. Joining the other messages in the rainbow of healing colors you create a divine symphony, empowering and transcendent.

This is the Miracle Healing you created. This is the healing gift you sent to Tom on March 29, 2009. This is the healing gift pre-sanctioned in the Presence of the Generous One, elevated to the station of Miracle Healing, which you asked me to bring back for you.

Best You Can

Do not become discouraged if your connection seems less vivid than mine. Your powers of access and recognition will grow and expand over time. Make this act of surrounding yourself in the Arc of Light and sending Tom healing in the Presence of the Generous One a daily practice. It will get so you can do this almost instantly by simply thinking of Tom and the rainbow of Miracle Healing.

Of course you may not want to hurry once you enter this blessed healing sanctuary. It does have a way of growing on you. Take the time to access the Arc of Light and send your Miracle Healing as often as you can. It takes six weeks of regular practice to form a shift in your consciousness, to develop a life habit, and in this case to embody the spirit of awesome power and beauty of the infinite. Send your healing message at a specific time of day. Choose a time. Remain consistent. Send your message daily. Living a life infused with the power of infinite abundance will rejuvenate and enliven every aspect of your life. Doing this in complete sincerity is a big step towards healing yourself from the plague of scarcity consciousness. Connecting to the Source of all that is will heal me and expand what you consider possible. It will expand what infinite possibility means for you.

We live in an ever-expanding universe. Your act of going into the Arc of Light with the intention of creating a Miracle Healing for Tom changes you. You are greater because of it. Your powers are greater. Your understanding is greater. Your vision is greater. Your consciousness is greater. And the universe is greater because of your vision, although you may not recognize these benefits at first. Processing such a dynamic change takes time.

Healing Is The Lodestone Of All Abundance

Your healing energy carries more than you think it does. It carries your hopes and dreams because it comes from you. It carries your energy. It was sent out of love without hope for personal gain, which gives your message the power of a fertile vision.

Jules Verne, a French author, had a vision of a nuclear powered submarine, the Nautilus. In 1870 he published what became a very popular book. It was his vision in an adventure book, *Twenty Thousand Leagues Under the Sea* (*Vingt Mille Lieues Sous Les Mers*,) eighty-four years before the world's first nuclear submarine, the *USS Nautilus,* was launched in 1954. His vision gave the scientists who designed it, the congressmen who funded it and the Navy brass who approved it an image of what was possible. His book created a vision that expanded the Universe.

Vision precedes the expansion of our physical reality.

Pablo Picasso painted figures and still life scenes using his vision of life showing all sides of an object at the same time. His cubist paintings depicted a view of life, which could only be seen by traveling at the speed of light. He did this as Albert Einstein was only beginning to postulate the effects of his world-changing *Theory of Relativity* and the reality-changing notion of traveling at the speed of light. Before then people had no concept of anything traveling at 186,286 miles per second, let alone imagining what life would look like at that speed.

His vision preceded the understanding and expansion of our physical reality.

Everyone said that harnessing the massive flow of the Colorado was impossible, until someone had the crazy idea it could be done using a massive labor force and a radical, new construction process. Franklin Delano Roosevelt, out of desperation to put people back to work in the USA in 1935, pushed through implementation of this impossible concept. The electricity from Hoover Dam gave both Las Vegas and Los Angeles the energy they needed to become powerful energetic cities.

Vision always precedes expansion of our physical reality.

These visions launched great change and benefit into our human experience. The greatest visions come from an evolved consciousness. That means your vision can exceed them all.

Your vision of a peaceful, loving world, a life of infinite abundance and a personal connection to your transcendent self is the ultimate healing possible in this world. It is why you came into this glorious time frame. This message you send back through the time-space matrix and into a different reality is monumental in the evolution of humankind, which you cannot fully appreciate, yet. Your vision bonded organically to your healing message is exceedingly important.

Those who do not share your vision for a more gentle and loving world, for a more prosperous healing experience for all humans are also projecting their visions. Visions bred in scarcity consciousness. These visions are affecting the reality of your world. They must not remain unchallenged as the only visions of your future.

Your healing messages are essential to our greater and lasting abundance. They carry with them the vibrations of your visions of peace, love and happiness and the Power and Might of all Creation.

Those negative visions vibrating toward greed, domination and separateness are not nearly as powerful as love, unity and divine inspiration. How can they be? Nothing is more powerful than your visions, which have been consecrated in the Presence of the Generous One.

New ideas, new concepts, new products, new methods – the expansion of our time-space matrix always begins with a vision. Oh, many have ideas about bigger and better things, but it is those connected few who have a vision and do something with it. They are the champions of our future. The question is are you willing to do nothing and allow the visions born of the scarcity consciousness to dominate your world? Your future? Your children's future? Or do you want your vision of a peaceful, loving, healing world to have a chance?

Start by using the template I offer until you become comfortable with it, then make your own. Continue to enter the Arc of Light and align with the Source of Creation whether Tom is still here in our current temporal matrix or not. Think of Tom as your body double. Remember separateness is a delusion of your consciousness. Tom, your loved ones, your pets, the lamp you are using, the book you are reading, these are all constructs you created. They are one with you. There is no difference healing Tom and healing those you love, because we are all one. Separateness is a delusion.

Send your healing to Tom because he marks one place where your Miracle Healing has already been granted. It has already been sanctioned in the Presence of the Generous One. Therefore it has no beginning and no ending. It exists within the infinite abundance of All-Creation. It is already a proven success and therefore the perfect training vehicle.

Remember Tom inside the Arc of Light, bathed in a living rainbow of Miracle Healing colors. Use that brilliant glowing rainbow as the visualization for Miracle Healing. Remember the Miracle Healing Rainbow and send a Miracle Healing message every single chance you get.

If you can't quite get your head around the universality of humankind, send your healing message anyway. Use wording that includes others you love. The form is not important.

Sending a healing message is important. Your visions are important. You are important.

We must create as individuals, not as sheep blindly following the ways of yesterday. *You are powerful beyond all measure.* If we are to heal our precious transformational playground and ourselves, we must do it as individuals. *You are powerful beyond all measure.* Strong, loving and inclusive. If we are to welcome in an era of world peace and universal prosperity we must do it with absolute sincerity and love. *You are powerful beyond all measure.* If we are to initiate an evolution of consciousness, an expansion of all that is possible, we must do it with the permission and acceptance of the Source of all that was, is and ever will be.

This may sound like a tall order, but I assure you it is not. Evolving this time-space matrix into a more peaceful, caring, honest, loving and healing environment begins by simply sending Tom Pauley a healing message back in the early morning hours of March 29, 2009.

Greatest Advantage Possible

I can't emphasize enough how important this one little act is. Not only for Tom, but also for you, all those you love and the earth itself. Doing this exercise opens the door to the greatest advantage anyone can hope to enjoy in this earthly experience.

You can do this. I know you can do this. Because you did it before. I was there. I watched you create my Miracle Healing. I received the Miracle Healing you created and I saw the results of your healing. I am alive, walking, talking, writing and enjoying my life because of the Miracle Healing you created. I am enjoying a full and complete recovery because of the Miracle Healing you created in the Presence of the Generous One.

Now is the time to take action again. Right now. Not in ten minutes. Not when you finish the book. Not when it is more convenient or quieter or more private. You must do something now. Again! Taking action immediately while you feel inspired is essential to the greatest successes in this temporal matrix. Because your inspired energy is inspiring. Just like touching a vibrating tuning fork to a non-vibrating tuning fork. You are at this very instant vibrating with the energy of creating a Miracle Healing.

Act now. Close your eyes and ask God to send Tom another healing message.

You cannot fail. Your success is guaranteed because you already have succeeded. Besides you have so very much to gain.

It Only Takes A Moment

Send Your Healing Message Again

You've already done this more than once. Now do it again. I was there. I saw first hand how strong and powerful your healing is.

1. Close your eyes and align with the Arc of Light.
2. Think of Tom Pauley back on March 29, 2009, in Saddleback Hospital needing your help.
3. Focus on that supernaturally brilliant rainbow of Miracle Healing in the Presence of the Generous One.
4. Gather a great force in your mind and speed your healing message on its way in your favorite color.
5. Detach and allow yourself to receive the revitalizing gift coming back to you. Notice how you feel. Staying open is essential.

Send Your Healing Message Now And Receive Your Gift Before Proceeding

CHAPTER 20

Your Miracle Healing

One of the most powerful features of sending your Miracle Healing while Tom is in the Presence of the Generous One, back in the early morning hours of March 29, 2009, is that you receive the gift you have long expected. You receive your own Miracle Healing, multiplied many times over. You may have already figured that out. I've talked about it for decades. Still I cannot emphasize it enough. This is one of the amazing features of this temporal time zone we call home. What you put out comes back multiplied. Because the Earthly experience is fecund. You plant a single kernel to grow a stock of corn yielding multiple ears each producing scores of kernels. Your supply of corn increases, greatly. The same applies to your growth. This is a Universal Law of our time-space continuum. Our actions as well as our thoughts are governed by Universal Laws. Laws as absolute as the Law of Gravity. Because of the Universal Laws of Reciprocation and Multiplication, if you think negative thoughts about someone you get that energy back affecting your life, multiplied. By virtue of those same Laws, when you think good thoughts about someone, you receive back into your life that same positive energy, multiplied many times over.

What To Expect

You sent me a Miracle Healing with a pure heart expecting nothing in return. This is vitally important. Because it is your selfless act of giving that initiates all the healing. Since you sent a healing message to Tom, you have received a Miracle Healing back to you, multiplied. Every time you send a Miracle Healing with no thought of personal gain you receive the same energy back to you. Greater than what you sent.

That is what you feel when you send your gift. You feel the rush of a Miracle Healing washing over you.

OK, you have received a powerful Miracle Healing. Now what? I'm sure you have a whole bunch of questions. Questions like, what should you expect? How soon should you expect it? If you have any current ailments or diseases, how soon should you expect those maladies to heal? Will you make more money or find a better job soon? When will you find your divine complement? Will it help you lose weight? Will you finally gain this relief or that fix? The questions go on forever.

These are all good questions. Questions I cannot answer. Because it's not that kind of healing.

The Miracle Healing, which you have received, has nothing whatsoever to do with healing, as you know it. You think of healing as a Band-Aid or a magic pill. Your Miracle Healing is not that. It requires a more mature understanding. It is not fixing something that is broken nor curing something that is diseased. It is not lowering your blood sugar nor keeping you from a heart attack. Of course, all that can clear up in the course of your Miracle Healing, depending upon your path. I have lower blood sugar numbers than ever before. In fact, the last time I went to my endocrinologist she said my numbers were so low I wouldn't be diagnosed as having diabetes today. Nine years ago my blood sugar numbers were a countdown to a stroke. Now they look fairly normal. My blood pressure is lower than all of my doctors'. My last reading was 117/61, down from 221/123, which was my reading the morning before my stroke. I'm taking the same medication or less than I was back then. I have gained a great physical healing in the past few years; that is undeniable. I am more centered emotionally than I have ever been. My mental progress is obvious. I am alive, standing, walking, eating, reading, writing and enjoying life. That has to count for something, right? I can only attribute these improvements in my health to my Miracle Healing. What I'm about to tell you is going to sound strange if not a tad bit confusing.

My Miracle Healing had nothing to do directly with my corporeal healing. The fact is, these human manifestations of physical, mental or emotional healing do not in any way do justice to the power and miracle of this unique and blessed gift I have been allowed to bring back for you.

The Miracle Healing, which you have chosen to accept, gives you a rare opportunity to reunite with that part of you that's been pulled apart and separated from you. It offers you a chance at making whole that part of you that has been misplaced. It is a unique opportunity for you to heal centuries of pain and conflict keeping you from your life's purpose and ultimate success in this blue marble in space-time.

Our current understanding of healing is immature. We are given illness and injury in this life so that we ask for healing. What you receive when you ask for healing is a re-establishing of the wholeness that is you. What you are seeking and what your Miracle Healing promotes is connecting you to your eternal transcendent self, so that you can become a more fully present version of who you really are. In this sense you cannot heal by yourself. This healing comes from your willingness to connect to your eternal transcendent self. Connecting and aligning with your eternal self who existed before you came into this world and will exist forever is the only way to access the power of this elevated understanding of Miracle Healing. You must align with the transcendent you that is one with the Source of all that is or ever will be.

Because what Miracle Healing really does is to align you with the Source of Creation.

Infinite Awareness of Creation

Your entire life on earth is a process in healing who you are. You are given challenges and obstacles that lead you to make choices from which there are always consequences. This gives you the impetus to become more in alignment with your eternal self so that you may understand your lessons in an elevated light. As you do this you become more fully aware of who you are. This is the golden ring, the divine union between you and your Transcendent Self, which is perfectly and permanently aligned with the Source of all that is.

This is the key to embodying the Infinite Awareness of Creation.

The connection to your transcendent self gives you an elevated perspective on your earthly experience. It helps you understand your own situation by providing a more complete awareness of the tests you are currently facing and their extended implications. Everyone is different in how you process this awareness. It gives you a chance to see, hear, know, feel or sense the machinations of the earthly experience with an understanding influenced by the wisdom of the infinite. It is like having access to a multi-dimensional hologram of your life's path. By grabbing that golden ring of the Infinite Awareness of Creation and connecting to your Transcendent Self frequently, you elevate your consciousness. By weighing your decisions using the scales of your eternal perspective against your earthly challenges you make better decisions. Decisions that lead you to more empowering consequences. Consequences that advance you faster and further along your path to the esteemed and elevated life you came here to enjoy. Think of this process as instantly acquiring a pro golf swing. Your ball drives straight and true off the tee farther than it ever has, eliminating time consuming and costly trips into the rough, the water and sand hazards or even, heaven forbid, completely out of bounds. Your golden ring helps keep you on a championship pace. You can also think of your connection to your Transcendent Self as one of those TV game shows where you can check with an outside source before you answer. Only this outside source is still you, an eternal and elevated version of you. It is a transcendent you that is one with the Source of all that is. Best of all this happens inside you effortlessly, organically. Talk about a win/win scenario!

You begin to see the world through a much clearer lens. Your reliance on separation fades as you rise to a greater, wider and more elevated perspective. You see a bigger part of the whole picture because you have come to possess a more highly elevated consciousness. With continued and regular connection, you come to exhibit the highest levels of action and leadership. The kind of leadership that you and those you love desperately need. This is the kind of leadership that remains serene under pressure and is not overly influenced by the emotion of the moment. The kind of leadership that opens doors to a higher level of creation and expansion. This, of course, makes for a far more joyful and abundant life.

All this comes from giving one glorious moment of your time while going about living your normal life.

Eventually, your golden ring of connection leads to the embodiment of an Infinite Awareness of Creation, which eliminates any possibility of holding a scarcity consciousness because you no longer see the consequences of this world in terms of lack. *Only takes a moment.* Embodying the Infinite Awareness of Creation allows you to grasp a bigger picture, a more elevated interpretation of your experiences.

Why would you fear loss of income or loss of love or poor health when you know deep in your being that this event is merely a transitional device designed to bring you to a fuller, more complete version of who you are? Why would you fear loss at all once you realize that your path is moving you to an even greater level of success and happiness, to a higher, more elevated station? Why would you fear any test once you know without a doubt that following your path and facing the tests and difficulties it holds is exactly what the transcendent you wants for you? How can fear exist when your elevated actions are exactly the actions you must take for your accession to the fulfillment of who you are?

As you heal you become more aware of your relationship with creation. The things that gave you concern yesterday will not give you concern today. Fear of lost income, fear of lost love and fear of tragic events yet to come will vanish in the fog of nothingness from which you have created them. Fear of failure, fear of success, fear of authority, fear of mistakes, fear of accidents, fear of war, fear of peace, fear of death, fear of living too long, fear of not living long enough, fear of pain, fear of pleasure, fear of sickness, fear of spiders, high places, low spaces, confined spaces – fear itself will cease to exist. Because you know as your Transcendent Self knows that you yourself control all such fears. You have created them and you can make them go away.

This is the nature of the gift of Miracle Healing you have received. You stop seeing scarcity and begin seeing opportunity. You stop feeling despair and begin feeling hope. You stop focusing on separateness and begin embracing unity.

When you encounter difficulties on your path be grateful. Tests and difficulties are given to you as a benefit for your growth. They give you the opportunity to expand yourself. Apparent hardships offer you the chance to create. *You are loved and protected at all times and under all conditions.* Creativity only occurs when there is limitation. Limitation requires you to be creative. You are given more opportunity to create when you are given limitation because you have to work around the obstacles. This is the very essence of creativity. Several of Van Gogh's most valued paintings present a ghostly appearance eliciting a faded or dreamlike quality. They stand in stark contrast to his vibrant work. I find them very compelling. They were painted during a period when he couldn't afford paint, so he got creative with the limitations he was given.

Face the tests and difficulties you encounter in life head on with the inspiration that comes from your Transcendent Self, and life will make you become the best possible version of yourself. The human experience will require you to become the highest most aligned version of who you are.

Otherwise you will be miserable. You will find an abundance of pain at every turn. This is not a threat because pain is not a punishment. Pain is simply a notice that you are not on your path. Much like the voice on your car's automatic guidance system telling you to turn around and return to the designated route as quickly as possible. Pain is telling you to stop what you are doing and align with your Transcendent Self as quickly as possible. Pain is a blessing.

I am sincerely grateful for all the pain I have received as a result of my stroke because of all it has led me to learn. It has taken away a smoldering misery, which lay hidden beneath a fog of deflection and denial. I have faced my pain and addressed defects I didn't realize I had, clearing my being of so much garbage. I am more content today than I have ever been. I know who I am.

You win either way. Pain can lead you to a clear and abundant life if you face your pain and address your defects. Or you can align with your Transcendent Self and get a little help along the way. Makes the journey so much more fun.

The quickest and surest way to align with your Transcendent Self is to send a Miracle Healing.

Sending this Miracle Healing is easier than waking to a beautiful spring sunrise. There is no downside to sending your healing message and the upside is infinite in the healing you generate.

Because you send this healing message of love you receive back a Miracle Healing multiplied many times over (Universal Law of Multiplication) each and every time you send one. *Only takes a moment.*

I actually get a rippling, healing vibration surging through my body after I send you a miracle healing. That feeling is wonderfully addicting. Best of all, you can have it anytime you want it all day long. *Only takes a moment.*

Because of the Miracle Healing, your consciousness will elevate. Instantly, your elevated consciousness will spread throughout the world. *Only takes a moment.* People you know, don't know, love and haven't yet learned to love will all be touched with the energy of pure healing. Little by little, they will begin vibrating at a higher rate. They will have their consciousness raised. Just like a vibrating tuning fork touching a non-vibrating tuning fork. Soon the entire world will vibrate at a higher rate.

Heal All By Healing One

This is why you send your Miracle Healing message. Yes, Tom needs it so he can come back and bring you this gift. Yes, the world and all you love need this healing. And yes, you, too, will receive a Miracle Healing. But let there be no mistake; this is not the primary reason you send your message back in time and into another universe. The reason you send this message must be to help someone else. This act must be selfless and absolutely cannot be fused to any desire for personal benefit or gain. You do it out of love. You do it because you can. You do it because we are all in this boat together. Because there is no such thing as separation – we are all one.

As a result of this selfless action you elevate your vibrational rate and the vibrational rate of humankind.

Because you have chosen to transverse the artificial bounds of time and space, because you have chosen to demonstrate your acceptance of infinite possibility as an actionable reality – you have expanded the Universe.

Because your gift and your intent are pure, you have connected to the good of all that is. You have connected to your Transcendent Self, allowing you to make that golden ring of connection, and opening the door to the Infinite Awareness of Creation.

Because making physical world choices in a state of alignment with the eternal is the path to elevating your eternal essence to the highest state of abundance possible in this time-space matrix. It is the path to becoming the elevated and enlightened soul you came here to become. It is the path to becoming the highest version of yourself you can become.

Imagine living a life where the Infinite Awareness of Creation consecrates everything you do, touch, feel, hold or share. Now, that's Rich Beyond Your Wildest Dreams. That's living a life filled with the greatest good imaginable. That's the essence of success and happiness.

This is what is meant by the evolution of your kind and your planet.

This is your Miracle Healing.

Regaining Your Perfection

When you were chosen to come into this world you were perfect. Birth and the process of becoming a functioning member of the human world forced you to forget all that you are, because you came here to struggle and grow. From the very beginning of your earthly experience, you have had the desire to possess your individualism. You learned to cry for attention. You learned how to get your own way. You learned how to get the things that served your earthly needs. As you advance to maturity, you take this knowledge and create the earthly life you desire.

You did all this in an immature state. The results are therefore spotty and incomplete much like the efforts of a teenager. Some of the things you do are elevated; some are not. Of course, you always grow and improve from the experience. The beauty of this gift is the opportunity it offers. It is a chance to make a quantum leap in your maturation.

Until now you have grown incrementally. This was acceptable in past time frames, but we are now at a critical juncture on the path of our human experience. The human stew of demands on the earth's resources together with the lopsided materialistic direction of the universal consciousness has brought the situation to a boiling point. At the risk of being labeled an alarmist I must clearly state: **Alarms are sounding**. Open yourself to them. Step away from the veil of deception and rationalization you have allowed to abridge your consciousness and block your understanding. Alarms are sounding everywhere. Louder than the storm and fire warnings you hear far too often these days. Louder than the declining options on the menu of your favorite seafood restaurant. Louder than the screams of conflict, hate and fear assaulting you daily from every corner of the globe. The alarms are warning you of the need for immediate action. They are trying to wake you out of your spiritual slumber even as you read these words. Eschew your preoccupation and your sole alignment with material wealth, which is at best temporary comfort destined to fade to the nothingness of another past life. This in no way precludes living a rich, happy and successful life. Seek balance. Align your consciousness with the ultimate success and perfectly balanced abundance of the Universe through your Transcendent Self.

This is how you attract your ultimate hopes and dreams. This is how you succeed in the face of overwhelming opposition and impossible odds. This is how you heal yourself and all you love from centuries of anger, greed and fear.

Remember, if the problem is not having enough, then the solution is incredibly simple: Connect to your transcendent self and seek an elevated life. Scarcity Consciousness cannot exist in a sea of infinite abundance.

We have reached the point of no return. It takes time to turn around the ecology and a culture of scarcity consciousness even with divine assistance. Healing requires organic changes because in this space-time matrix everything happens organically. Ours is a fertile matrix whose very nature depends of the ability to grow and reproduce. This requires a verdant and viable, life sustaining eco-system. For us to have the opportunity to grow and expand we must have a planet that can grow and expand. Unless we take the first steps now, we stand the risk of starting too late.

Time is short.

Scarcity consciousness is your obstacle. It is your challenge. Seize your opportunity to create a world you love to call home.

Once you grab hold of that gold ring of union between your human experience and your Transcendent Self, the worldwide healing will progress faster than the speed of light because you will heal faster than the speed of light. Improvements that previously may have taken a generation will become practically instantaneous. The hopes and dreams of humanity for millennia will find realization before your eyes. As you continue to grow and elevate you will organically send this radiant living gift of Miracle Healing to those you love and to those you do not yet love, and our numbers will grow. More and more humans of all ages, races, cultures, genders, languages, capacities and beliefs from every segment of society will join us on that pier. They will climb from the chaos without knowing why. They will join us in sending their healing message of love to help another. Eventually, the storms of scarcity consciousness will subside and a more universally just and loving world will grow in its stead. Only then can you and all that you love live in a state of peace and create the thriving, joyous life you came here to enjoy.

The happy and bountiful life you dream of having cannot be bought, sold, demanded, decreed, manipulated, negotiated nor forced in any way. You cannot make it happen. You must receive and allow. Your happy and bountiful life is given to you. It is a gift and a birthright of the human experience. The anxiety and conflict inherent in scarcity consciousness pushes this cherished prize away. Your hopes and dreams can flourish only in a state of peace, love and acceptance. To live the rich life you came here to live, seek peace and love above all else. Your ultimate success depends on having peace in your personal life and peace in the lives of all your brothers and sisters throughout the world. There is no such thing as separation. It is a delusion of an immature consciousness. There are no they and we. There are no good guys and bad guys. There are no winners and losers. *We are one.* Your difficult neighbors are simply another side of you. *We are one.* What happens in Africa or Columbia or the Middle East happens to you. When they bleed you bleed. *We are one.* The effects of hunger, hatred and war do not stop at county lines, border crossing or oceans. *We are one.* They affect your consciousness as surely as 9/11 affected the world consciousness.

The deleterious effects of scarcity consciousness hinder your well being regardless of where, when or to whom they occur. It diminishes your birthright. When fear of not having enough holds you back, your growth and advancement is retarded. It brings you less, not more; it prevents you from living the bounteous life you deserve to live. The life you asked to live.

You can grow and change here. You cannot do that in the next life. You can expand your consciousness and create here. You cannot do that in the next life. Here you can grow and expand yourself and the Universe as you know it. You can become the whole and complete essence of being your soul sought in coming here. This is the star-studded golden ring of all that can be desired.

Imagine this! You can actually change reality. You can cause the entire universe to grow and expand to a degree that would have been thought impossible only moments before. On a moonless night on a dark mountain highway I created a real life impossibility. I created a living breathing Jackalope.

What will you create?

I have been telling you forever that you came here to learn and grow, but that's not the whole story. You came here to expand the Universe. Because as you grow and expand so does the Universe. So do all your fellow travelers on this speck of matter-based possibility. You did not come for the transitory goals and desires of this training ground, this temporal anomaly. That is just the game we all play to reach that top prize, that gold ring of divine union. You came for the opportunity to play and grow. What you ultimately desire is the strength, the power, the infinite grace, beauty and glory of the wholeness of being.

The gift this book offers you is far beyond the bounds of your current human experience. Once you cross that threshold of our time-space matrix back on March 28, 2009 and enter the Court of the Presence of the Generous One in my nanoseconds of dire need, your message will instantly be granted the power of Miracle Healing. You will become a Miracle Healer. Your particular manifestation of this station depends on your path. Maybe you will initiate Miracle Healing among traders on Wall Street. Or along the corridors of power in your government. Or among your family and friends. Or in the backwaters of the Mississippi or the Nile or the Huang He. Maybe it will lead to more peaceful and loving business practices. Maybe it will lead to halting the mass destruction of our environment. Maybe it will lead to a union and a new child being born who is needed now. More likely, you'll never know where your Miracle Healing leads. You have no way of knowing what your ultimate path is or where it will take you. Let alone someone else's. This is the adventure of life on earth. This is the joy of life in this precious transformational playground. Wherever it takes you, rest assured that your path leads to the answer to that most important and all-important question, the question that unlocks and endows your life with the Infinite Awareness of Creation.

Who am I?

CHAPTER 21
The Rest Of The Story

Now that you have sent me your gift of Miracle Healing I can tell you a little about my stay in Acute Recovery. I couldn't tell you about my stay before this. I tried several times to no avail. The words just wouldn't flow. When I tried to force them they came out all wrong, sad and angry. I had to wait until I had written the chapter telling you how to send your healing gift into another dimension and back into a different time frame.

Since we live in a time-space continuum there is no flow of time. Time is permanently tied to the function of space. We are not a thousand years removed from the Crusades; we are simply more mature, more elevated and living in a more enlightened time-space. The fact that you can go backwards in time to correct pain from your own past or to send a healing message to me in the early morning hours of March 29, 2009 is a testament to this space-time effect. It is a testament to the construct of the world in which we live. This is very important to remember if you want to gain any significant degree of mastery over your human experience.

A further extension of our space-time matrix applies to this book I am currently writing and you are currently reading. It exists in published form for you to buy and read the instant I finish writing it. Energy-wise, there is little difference between the time frame in which I have a finished manuscript and the one where you are reading these pages in book format. Each chapter I finish makes the eventuality of a finished book more real, more certain I will produce a finished manuscript and that manuscript will be published. This makes the energy of each chapter more powerful and more potent in your present time frame. I know it sounds a little counter to the reality we meet every single day of our lives. That quantum reality, time-space matrix thing takes some getting used to.

You've already proven your continued healing prowess. I'm much stronger today than when I started writing. In fact, after I finished the "Deliverance" chapter my healing jumped tenfold. I was able to face one of the more arduous challenges of my life. It was the part of my recovery, which ultimately allowed me to bring my efforts in writing this book to a conclusion. Completing what you start is always the hardest part. It is the manifestation of your vision. The more ambitious and elevated your vision the more difficult the conclusion. Which is why it may have been difficult for you to take one tiny moment to send your healing back to me. Not because the action itself was trying, but because you were bringing your efforts to a conclusion.

All I'm saying is: Keep an open mind. You can do this. You can heal so much more than me. I've seen the storm calm and the waters recede.

I hope you will take from this book the tools and encouragement to elevate your consciousness and thereby your personal power. Lift yourself above the mundane physical reality demanding your attention and create a Miracle Healing. *Only takes a moment*. Abandon the common wisdom of your day, expand

and enrich the Universe in a positive way for yourself and for all of humankind.

Taking time out from your busy day to call the Arc of Light into your life is fantastically healing on both spiritual and mundane levels, as we have shown. The mundane healing of allowing your body a spiritual refresher alone is worth the time. Meditating has shown to lower your chances of high blood pressure, high blood sugar and a bevy of other purely awful physical problems. I wish I had welcomed the calming effects of inviting the Arc into my life before my stroke because the Arc increases this meditating effect at least a trillion fold.

Back to the energy of completion and how it works: I had to write the previous chapters before telling you about my stay in Acute Rehab because I couldn't have had a recovery until I had received your gift of Miracle Healing. And you couldn't send your gift until I'd written the chapters telling you how and why to send it. I know it doesn't seem to make a lot of sense, because obviously I did have a stay in Acute Rehab or I couldn't be here writing about it. That's the problem with a quantum reality. When the cause comes after the effect, it flies in the face of common wisdom.

A Ming Vase

It's exactly the same as my Living Videos. I couldn't see the end of my children's journey. I couldn't see my wife's life to the end. I couldn't see the gift I was holding up to calm the terrible storm, which was destroying everything I loved. It was not that I wasn't allowed to see it. It was simpler than that. It was not possible for me to see those things because the cause that affected and forged those events had not yet occurred. The kids had not faced their challenges, chosen and grown from the consequences of their action. Diane had not faced, chosen and grown from hers. I had not made a final decision to go on or to stay. Even though I could see part of the future I could only see so far because the future is not set until you create it. The Universe that held those futures, the kids, Diane's and mine, had not been created yet. The beautiful gift I held up, we held up, against the storms of separation, fear and anger, didn't exist, couldn't exist until I decided to stay in this temporal matrix and write this book. Then only as the manuscript reached completion could it become the brilliantly gleaming divine gift, which inspired us to quiet the raging storms of scarcity consciousness. Think of it as a video of a gorgeous Ming vase at the beginning of movie, fading up from complete darkness and shining brighter and more distinct until the fade up is complete and the movie begins.

This also means that the healing effect of your gift is affecting the world as a whole already as the manuscript nears completion. Even though you have not read a single word.

There must always be a cause before there can be an effect. Even if the cause comes after the effect. I know it sounds just a little bit convoluted, but it is absolutely, positively, one hundred percent true.

Toilet Seat Covers

After I'd written Quantum Selling, I went back to the Monroe Institute in Virginia. That's where Robert Monroe trained the remote viewers for the U.S. Army Stargate Project back in the last part of the 20th century. Today they teach a variety of seminars to folks like you and me using his methods. In case you aren't familiar with remote viewing or the Stargate Project, they were psychic spies. Remote viewers would lie on a couch in an Army base in Virginia, and using only the power of their minds, "remote view" a specific target anywhere in the world. The absolute best intelligence the U.S. received during the first Gulf War came from remote viewers. It was so good, eventually knowledge of this top-secret project leaked out. The media became aware that Congress was using psychic spies. It made for great TV, but not good politics. The idea that Congress was using public money, "taxpayers' hard earned dollars," on something as seemingly ungodly, heretical and just down right controversial as psychic spies doesn't play well among many voters. Congress did the only politically correct thing they could do. They immediately stopped funding the project, disbanded the remote viewers and publicly condemned the whole affair as an abomination to all God-fearing folk. To this day, both Congress and the Army refuse to admit publically there ever was a Stargate Project. Of course, the project was so successful that they simply renamed it, hired and trained new remote viewers and buried the cost in that huge military budget, probably under toilet seat covers.

I went to the Monroe Institute to see if I could pick up anything I could use in Quantum Selling. Now, theirs is obviously a good program and it works, but I felt it was a little behind the curve, at least, for my purposes. It is over thirty years old. The one thing I did gain was that the viewers needed to see the follow-up or feedback at the conclusion of the event they viewed. They needed to see pictures of whatever they had viewed after their intelligence was acted upon. If they viewed missile sites they needed to see the video the bombers made when the bombs were dropped. Because the remote viewers were actually viewing the pictures they were shown afterward, not the place itself. They still viewed the future, but it was a future that had already been created. They viewed the effect of the cause they were helping to create.

The bottom line is, we live in a cause and effect quantum reality. The laws of our time-space matrix are absolute. Once again, because heaven forbid you forget:

There must always be a cause before there can be an effect. Even if the cause comes after the effect.

You probably thought you were picking up a book of light reading about how pretty it is in the next life. Maybe confirm your own preconceived notions about heaven, which by the way are probably true. Your thoughts are expanding the Universe daily. You can have anything you want in this life. Why not have the next worlds be of your choosing, too? When I started this project I thought I was writing a book about the pretty things I saw. At least, my conscious mind thought that. Deep down somewhere inside the hidden caverns of my subconscious I think I knew this book opened doors to possibility most, including me, had not seriously considered. That's probably why I tried to avoid writing it. I never considered the extent to which this book was about the unexplored mysteries of our short and exciting life here in this wonderfully precious transformational playground we call earth.

I am, however, constantly drawn to new doors in want of opening. Being the curious guy that I am, I open them. What am I to do? They call to me. You can understand that, can't you? You were drawn to this book. You opened it and now here you are, considering things that would have earned you a trip to a funny farm or at least a visit to a shrink in a bygone era. Of course, as you well know by now, there is no such thing as time. You live in a time-space continuum and that distinction has a very powerful effect on your day-to-day life. This powerful effect creates an opportunity for unimaginable abundance.

This is all so exciting. Just think about the power you hold in your mind right now. Go ahead flex your power. Close your eyes and imagine Tom in the Presence of the Generous One and create another healing message of pure love right now. *Only takes a moment.* It'll come right back to you, multiplied many times over.

CHAPTER 22
Back To Rehab

I was starting to tell you a little about my experience in Acute Rehab. Two days after I had the tryout in ICU, pulling my weakened and paralyzed body up on the apparatus, I was moved to a private room in Acute Rehab. How I ended up in the only private room I cannot explain. It was probably another benefit of your Miracle Healing. Or perhaps it was a gift from God to the other patients in the recovery unit. I was not in the best of spirits. Once I fully realized how difficult my situation was I came out fighting mad. Irish mad! If I could have thrown stuff I'm sure I would have. The tomato soup was mostly an accident. I definitely would not have made a very good roommate.

Everybody in Acute Rehab dealt with his or her fate differently. But there's one thing I can guarantee, no one saw his or her difficulty as a God given opportunity to grow and expand the Universe. Certainly nobody was singing praises and thanking God for the difficulties they faced. Often our greatest gifts seem a lot like punishment. Most came in feeling sorry for themselves. Like they had accepted that they were destined to spend the rest of their life with less than before. They were learning how to cope.

I admit that thought definitely crossed my mind. I was angry, sure, which I blame entirely on the second stage of grief. Still, I had a different mindset. I was there to get my life back. My first stage, denial, was working overtime because I tried not to think about what I'd lost. Oh, I had my moments. Late at night when I couldn't sleep I'd cry for my past life. But for the most part, I was determined to get my life back on track, fast. I was not about to settle for that scarcity consciousness crap. I had been promised a full and complete recovery and, by God, I would have it! My death experience had made such an impact on me I woke every day with the absolute clarity that my full and complete recovery was guaranteed. All I had to do was give 110% every waking minute. I was impatient with any delay and absolutely determined to move forward with all due haste.

Apparently, that attitude came off a tad bit edgy to those around me. I tended to rub people the wrong way at times. I did manage to offset my ill humor by using my natural born wit and charm. It worked, too. I know because I overheard one therapist complimenting me to another therapist one day. She said, "Oh yeah. He can be quite charming when he isn't yelling at you!"

Full And Complete Recovery Guaranteed

It took all the strength I could muster to climb out of bed that first day. I had lots of help, don't get me wrong, but just clambering out of bed was exhausting. The right side of my body was of no help whatsoever. It was totally paralyzed. Every movement was excruciatingly difficult. I had to pick up and carry my right arm and leg with my left hand. Getting out of bed I had to reach over and pick up my right leg and move it, then pick up my right arm and move it. Over and over again. Out of the bed, I had to manually position my right leg and arm so I could get into the wheelchair. Once in the chair I had to pick up my right arm, which was always just hanging down and set it on the arm of the wheelchair. The whole time my right shoulder screamed how unhappy it was, because the muscles that held that arm in place didn't work anymore and my shoulder was pulling apart. I grabbed my right leg to get it on the footrest and lifted my right arm onto the oversized armrest that held it in place. Neither of my limbs was much interested in cooperating. Boy, that gets old darn quick. I was pushing, pulling and prodding over 100 pounds of dead weight every inch of the way. Eventually, I got angry with my own body for not helping, for just hanging there. Getting dressed, climbing out of bed and getting into a wheelchair felt like a major accomplishment. I was ready to call it a day right there and then. The nurse helping me quickly reminded me it was 6:00 a.m. and I had a full day of rehab ahead.

"Fun, fun, fun 'til daddy took the T-Bird away, now."

Rehab wasn't fun, but I was grateful I had the chance. The chance I got because you gave me the gift of Miracle Healing.

Finger Of Hope

Just to be clear, I was pretty much a lump of half paralyzed clay. I needed a lot of help making my recovery a reality. There were three kinds of rehab, each requiring a specialist: the physical therapist, the occupational therapist, and the speech therapist. Well, four, if you count the shrink. I didn't pay much attention to him. I guess I was kind of insulted the doctors would think I needed any kind of mental adjusting. Why in the world would I need mental adjusting? I had to push and prod my weakened and paralyzed body to work again. That's all. I grew up in Nebraska. Hard work is in my DNA. Work and work hard, that's all I needed to focus on. "Just, git 'er done!" It was my body that needed fixing, not my mind. Who ever heard of such a thing? There was nothing wrong with my mind! OK, I had a hole in my brain the size of a racket ball, but I wasn't focusing on that. I had work to do.

I was definitely in denial. It was three years before I finally dragged my backside to a psychologist. Believe me, I needed her help. Besides, she was young, really good looking and was a Dead Head in her misspent youth. Who wouldn't need that?

The occupational therapist in Acute Rehab prepared me for my coming out party by teaching me practical things like brushing my teeth, getting dressed and strengthening my arm and my dexterity. Since my arm and fingers didn't move at all she couldn't do much there. We did go through the motions. Strapping my arm and hand to various contraptions and sundry exercises. The mind has to know what you want it to do before it can accomplish the task. Apparently, the arm and fingers are the last to improve. By the time I went home I could move the tip of my index finger of my right hand about one-eighth of an inch. Wow! What an upper it was to move that one finger. I remember sitting in my wheelchair, watching my finger every morning and knowing my Miracle Recovery had begun. I actually looked forward to waking up to see how far my finger moved each day.

All Strokes Are Different

Oh, my occupational therapist also gave me showers and helped me dress for the day. She made sure I could tell the difference between armholes in my tee shirts and the openings in my shoes and what to do with each. Don't laugh! Some folks couldn't do that. It was amazing how differently people were affected by their brain damage. One guy came out relatively unscathed except for the fact he lost his ability to speak, completely. He couldn't even make basics sounds. Another lady couldn't walk or remember her family. She remembered everybody else, but not her family. Most people were older than I was. Except, for one pretty young woman home from college for Spring Break. She was 19. She drove a little too fast through a state park one night and crashed her brand new sports car into a stately hundred-year-old Live Oak at 50 miles an hour. The good news was that the tree was not badly damaged. The car, however, was totaled. Miraculously, the girl came away with no broken bones or ripped skin. The bad news was brain damage. For two days she ran around Acute Rehab day and night in her underwear, demanding to go home. It was not a pretty sight. Dr. Kenneth Lynn, the director of Acute Rehab told me about a similar case. The man could function quite well, but he had lost his ability to act on what he saw. He could see cars coming down a street, for example, know that they were dangerous and could hurt him, but he'd walk out in the street anyway. His wires to act upon danger signals were permanently disconnected. He'd have to have someone watch him twenty-four seven for the rest of his life. No matter how bad we think we have it, things could always be worse. At least, we'd consider them worse. We can't judge the tests and difficulties of others from our own perspective. It's their chance to choose, experience the consequences and grow and expand. I can only express how grateful I am for my Miracle Healing. This whole experience has been plenty to accept and grow from.

Thank you. Thank you. Thank you for your gift of Miracle Healing.

The speech therapist worked on my speech as you might expect. At that time frame the right side of my face just hung there in a death mask frown. My vocal cords and the muscles governing my ability to speak and swallow were also affected. All they gave me were thickened liquids and Jell-O for I don't know how long. If your throat doesn't close off the airway to your lungs every time you swallow then you can aspirate, opening yourself to pneumonia. Still, I was ready to organize a raiding party on the food cart by the time I tasted real water, ice tea and graham crackers and cream cheese. Bagels were not on the menu.

My speech therapist made me work my voice and throat muscles when I couldn't even gargle decently, but I got stronger. My face gradually came back. It took over a year of doing those exercises before that death mask thing was gone. I liked my speech therapist. As a wedding present I gave her a floral painting I made with my left hand during my stay in Acute Recovery. She fell in love with the painting. I thought Diane was going to strangle me when she found out. I guess she liked it too. I painted her a bigger one once I got back home. It's kind of a modified Jackson Pollack/impressionist version of my prized yellow and orange hibiscus, Hawaiian Sunset.

Reconnecting Daily

Every morning and evening I would go to my room and spend time in the Portal drawing healing energy from the quantum side. At least, that's what I thought I was doing in that time frame. Now, I'm not so sure. I was probably accessing that instant when I was awash with the rainbow of Miracle Healing colors you sent. Back then I was numb from the whole experience and I was sort of running on cruise control. I was used to doing the Quantum Selling exercises; they came without thinking which was a good thing. Either way, I would see a particular color envelop my body. Every time I did this the color changed, which lends credibility to the idea that I was reconnecting to my Miracle Healing. I am convinced that discipline was of great aid and benefit to my healing, both in assisting with my recovery and in giving me the reassurance I needed to continue the daily grind of doing the impossible, waking unresponsive body parts and building new neuro-pathways.

This is exactly what you can experience in those precious healing moments immediately after you send your healing message to Tom and the world. As you remember, once you create a Miracle Healing of pure love you receive one back, multiplied. It is in those oh so precious moments that you can soak up the same incredible healing energies I did and still do. I encourage you again to remain in alpha, open to receive the entire good coming to you after you send your healing message.

I continued this practice for years after I left the hospital. In fact, for three years I couldn't do anything in the Portal except call healing energies to my body. After breakfast I would go out back on our portico and sit in my camp chair, close my eyes and go into the Portal. I would see healing energies flow through my body. By then they were either streams of electric cornflower blue or waves of intensely soothing sea-foam green. Sometimes I would see bolts of healing energy hitting me like lightening. They were an array of different colors and frequencies. An amazingly intense and powerful red, a constantly moving and surging indigo in various textures and tones, a purple so soothing and peaceful, yellows so light and funny I always smiled, all alive and teeming with healing properties. These bolts of healing energies would roll down my holographic body bringing healing to the places that needed them. I would always feel a shudder of electricity running down my spine when the bolts hit. Other times I would focus the healing lightening on my brain and visualize new neural pathways forming. They'd always appear – maybe, the best way to explain it in our color spectrum is a living, breathing, day-glow orange. I'd watch these sentient colors move like a CGI of a car traveling across a map of the USA. They'd travel from my brain down my spine to a junction, then down my arm or leg. It was really cool. I'd get caught up in that and lose all track of time. As I have here.

Without one single doubt, my training in the Portal prepared me for my recovery. It gave me a leg up, a head start on my personal healing. It was such a comfort knowing I could affect change and healing in my body by using the pathway of my mind. Nothing happens to us that isn't something we can handle.

I Couldn't Tell Them

Oh, I have been able to get back functions like crossing my right leg over my left leg without using my hands. It took a lot of hard work and the help from Dr. Clay Miller, one of my chiropractors. He uses a unique nerve and muscle bundle massage technique he developed. He engendered amazing results. It floored my stroke doctor, Dr. Lynn, when I showed him my new skill three years later. He looked up at me with an expression of deeply felt surprise and said, "Well, I guess you can get back function after a year."

Again, thank you all for my Miracle Healing. I believe it keeps working because you keep sending your messages. I hope you keep sending them long after I'm gone. Sending your healing message back in time and into another dimension where I received your healing will remain a doorway to a guaranteed path to Miracle Healing regardless of whether I'm on this physical plane or not. This opportunity for expansion exists for all time. Keep that Miracle Healing of rainbow colors in your mind.

Walking exercises were done in the hallway outside my room. The goal was for me to walk 100 feet before I went home. The exercise initially took two therapists. One to push the wheelchair behind me, so when my legs would inevitably give out and I'd fall from exhaustion I could fall back into the chair. The other therapist would walk backward in front of me holding my hemi-walker and spouting encouragements with my every movement. Learning to walk again was incredibly difficult. First of all, the only way I could get my right leg to function in a way that even approximated walking was to throw it forward using my right hip. It was not possible to lift my leg at all. The first day I tried walking, I managed to take almost three steps before I was too worn out to continue and had to go back to my room for a nap. It was more than physical exhaustion. My brain was exhausted, too. By the end of the first week I was taking five steps. My encourager was legitimately shocked with my progress. She kept repeating, "I can't believe you. Your will is so strong. By all rights you shouldn't be able to do this. You shouldn't be able to walk at all."

It wasn't only my encourager who was amazed at my recovery. The whole staff told me how unbelievable my recovery was. Nobody said it, but they all knew I should be dead or at least in long-term bed rest. I think the doctors ultimately allowed me to go to Acute Rehab to simply quiet Diane and Penelope.

There were plenty of Code Blues while I was there. Every one reminded me I had chosen to return which spurred me onward. The doctors, therapists and nurses who treated me couldn't seem to get over my amazing recovery. I was a bit of a hero 'round those parts. In my exit conference the whole staff, one by one, told my family what a marvel I was. The head physical therapist, the same one that originally brought the apparatus into ICU and gave her approval for my admittance to Acute Recovery said, "Tom has made the most amazing recovery of any patient we have ever had. His strong will and positive attitude has worked nothing less than a miracle."

She didn't understand. None of them did. And I couldn't tell them. I was still processing everything myself. The fact was my miracle recovery wasn't because of me. It was because of you. I had been given the gift of Miracle Healing. My recovery was guaranteed from the start. All I had to do was put in the work. Just think about that for a second. If you knew you had a Miracle Healing, if you knew your healing was absolutely, divinely guaranteed, no matter what the difficulty was, trauma, illness, substance abuse, economic troubles, marital strife, persistent unhappiness, wouldn't you act differently? If all you had to do to overcome your illness were to put in the work, wouldn't you approach your life with more enthusiasm? More confidence. More certainty. More "l'amour de la vie."

Your Guaranteed Recovery

Think about it! Imagine if you lost all your money. Maybe you lost your job. Or you were taken to the cleaners in a business deal. Or you were abused in some unspeakable manner. Maybe you lost your home to the bank. Or you lost your spouse to someone else. Or you suffered great mental, emotional or physical loss. Or you were diagnosed with some supposedly terminal disease. Sure, you'd go though all the stages of grief. Then you'd have to recover or die. Difficulties can be a living death when you feel sorry for yourself, give up and live a life of regret and failure. The buried anger alone would make your life hell on earth. Unless you stand up, face your pain and do something about it. You could blame God, yourself or someone else for your difficulties. What profit is there in that? You'd miss the lesson! You'd lose out on the growth! You'd lose your shot at Infinite Awareness of Creation!

Ask yourself: How would I handle my recovery if I knew without a shadow of a doubt that my difficulties were for my highest good? That they were given to me at my request? That they were an opportunity instead of a punishment? That I would come out stronger, richer, happier and more powerful than ever once I faced them?

You'd handle your test differently, right? Don't you think everybody would? Remember, in this time-space matrix what you put out comes back multiplied. You sent Tom a Miracle Healing of pure love consecrated in the Presence of the Generous One. That means you, too, have received back a Miracle Healing, which is guaranteed. The only difference is your healing is multiplied many times over. The more you send the more you receive back.

Put in the work! Your full and complete recovery is absolutely positively guaranteed.

Here's Your Challenge

How will you approach life now? As you send Tom and others a Miracle Healing of pure love, how will you think, feel and act then? Will you become as determined to have your healing as I was? Will you look at financial downturns, lost jobs and busted economies as an opportunity to grow, learn and expand? Will you take your shot to become more than you were? Will you act with confidence, determination and love of life when your health or life is threatened or when you have to deal with discrimination or loss? Or when you have not yet found the love of your life or the success you desperately hope to find? If, God forbid, your recovery requires you must learn how to walk or feed yourself again maybe using artificial limbs, what will you do?

Will you look at the myriad of tests and difficulties you face in your path as an opportunity to grow, learn and expand yourself and the Universe? Will you cherish your short time in this earthly experience and make the most of it? Every single minute of every single day! Will you take the high road? Will you love others? Will you love your enemies? Will you treat the world with kindness and charity? Will you treat others as you yourself would be treated? Will you press onward when the swords flash? Will you move forward when the shafts fly? Will you stand up and be counted when your path leads you to seemingly impossible choices and seemingly unwinnable scenarios?

You are the one! This is your time. This is your one and only chance to do the job, to live the life you came here to live.

Will you join me on that pier and face the storms of destruction laying waste to our precious transformational playground? **Your transformational playground. Your life! Your future! Your happiness and abundance!**

Will you stand firm against the onslaught of naysayers and those who would have you follow the ephemeral precepts and desires of a deathly ill civilization?

Will you seek connection and alignment with your Transcendent Self and the Source of all that is, was or ever will be? Will you continue to send healing messages of pure love into the Presence of the Generous One? Will you put in the work?

This is now your challenge. This is how you evolve to the next level of possibility. This is how you grow, expand and create a loving peaceful world for yourself and all that you love. Oh, it's not the only path, but this path is simple and guaranteed.

This is your mission. Not mine. Mine was to write a book and keep teaching. That's what I do. You'll have to do what you do. You'll have to do it with an unabridged consciousness and a pure heart if you want to enjoy all the Good you have so long dreamed about and prayed the All-Powerful Forces of Creation to bring. If you really want to enjoy a Miracle Healing, you have to choose to accept it every single day for the rest of your life.

I know you can do it. You've done it before. I've seen you do it. You were amazingly brilliant. I cannot say it enough. You were brilliant and successful. But you still have to choose to do it. You must decide.

This is not the easiest way to spend your life. It is simply an incredibly rewarding and fulfilling avenue to living a life of Infinite Abundance. I have found it makes my life a great adventure for which I can be proud. It is a life filled with challenges and opportunities I can face with enthusiasm and integrity. Why not? I'm loved and protected at all times and under all conditions.

Join The Evolution

In all honesty, I must admit I have not always made the most of the opportunities I've been given in my life. Nobody's perfect. His Holiness Christ, Mohammed and Baha'u'llah left the growing reality of what they saw on their path, their mission and retreated to the desert to find the strength to deal with what was coming for them. The Bab was imprisoned in the mountains of northern Iran where He prepared Himself for His martyrdom. Moses wandered in the desert for forty years. I'm not sure about the other Manifestations of God like Krishna, Buddha, Zoroaster and The Great Spirit. I am sure they, also, faced choices and consequences they would rather not have faced. As His Holiness Christ said, "O Lord, let this cup pass from me."

It's only natural and frankly expected that we try to avoid brick walls in our path, which is why it is so very important you send out a Miracle Healing every chance you get. It gives you a leg up, a heightened perspective, the expansive and evolved power of a transcendent being. We are here in this life to face tests and difficulties, make choices and grow from the consequences. That's it. That and have fun. The best rejuvenator in this life, the best supercharger, the best secret power to moving forward with gusto toward success in this life, is having fun. Fun combines joy with detachment, both of which you need to heal and overcome the challenges you face.

Remember you only face the obstacles you can overcome. Obstacles designed expressly for you, for your benefit, for your healing and transcendence. You're not charged with bringing a new era of enlightenment into the world like Manifestations of God. You are merely asked to do the best you can. To grow and expand the Universe you live in by living the life you came here to live. To elevate yourself and to love all you see in this life because it is all truly a divine gift to us. Above all, you must avoid a scarcity consciousness and refuse to see life though the eyes of defeat, mistake and failure. They are lies, horribly destructive illusions. You don't need them. Strive always to align yourself with the higher order of possibility. Embrace goodness, fairness and honesty, knowing you are loved and protected at all times and under all conditions.

This is how you heal from the slings and arrows of outrageous fortune. This is how you elevate your consciousness and heal yourself and all you love from the self-defeating effects of a scarcity consciousness. This is the gift that quiets the raging storms and heals the earth. This is the path to living a life of Infinite Abundance.

Evolution into an elevated, unabridged consciousness is the next big challenge you face. We face. We few. We incredibly lucky few who have been chosen to breathe the air and walk the paths given us in this life, in this amazing time of change and transformation. This time frame in which you live is the most important period of change in the history of our civilization. This is why you connect with your Transcendent Self.

This is how you answer for yourself that all important question, "Who am I?" This is how you embody the Infinite Awareness of Creation. This is how you clothe yourself in the endless bounty of All-Creation.

This is how you evolve. This is how you evolve. This is how you evolve.

Join us in the Evolution of Humankind and the salvation of our precious transformational playground, planet earth.

I need you. The world needs you. You and all that you have ever loved or will ever love need you.

Thank you, once again, for everything you do, have done and will ever do.

See you on the pier, brothers and sisters.

See you on the pier.

Hummingbird

One incredibly beautiful early spring morning back in Southern California, I went out on my back portico to call in the Arc of Light and send a Miracle Healing to all of you. The sky was clear blue. The temperature was about 75 degrees Fahrenheit. I could smell a touch of sea air perfumed with the fragrance of the spring flowers already in full bloom. I was in a sensational mood. Home in a paradise of color and beauty. I was living my dream. A pair of Red-Tailed Hawks had nested in the tree above me. Their chicks would hatch any day now and start demanding food, filling my yard with the happy sounds of new life. God was in his heaven. Everything was going right in my world.

As I entered the Arc, all the sounds of the world around me seemed to vanish. I could hear a faint melody reminiscent of the angel music that welcomed me once before. When I recognized what the melody was, I released all control, simply accepted the coming vision and relished the moment. Totally lost in the moment, I saw in my mind's eye an overview of the earth. I could see the earth rotating as though I was positioned in satellite orbit. At the same time, I could see close ups of the cities and countryside. I saw people working and playing in total peace and happiness.

The coastal formations of the continents were different. The sea had risen. The coastal cities were smaller and farther back from the seas. All across the planet the smaller, yet flourishing human population had spread out into the countryside. Everywhere I looked I saw a verdant and healthy environment. Brimming with foliage and wildlife. The Amazon seemed to have grown and expanded. The jungles of Southeast Asia and Africa were also thriving, smaller, but growing and expanding. Many new cities, circular and smaller in design, occupied the interior of the continents. Even the deserts showed renewed vigor and life. A great deal of agriculture was going on there. I was overcome with joy when I realized the deserts were blooming.

There was more water than there is now. More lakes and bigger oceans, and very small permanent ice deposits. The climate seemed to be more temperate. Large clear protective domes covered what must have been the business districts of the cities. The people were exceedingly happy and void of any apparent stress. Definitely not overworked. If anything, they seemed to spend their days mostly playing, as did the laughing, happy children. I didn't feel the crying need in the world for food and substance I do now. There was no great feeling of want at all. Most rewarding of all, there was neither the slightest hint of volatile anger nor the machinery of war. Peace was by far the overriding ambience across the entire globe.

I caught myself wondering if this vision was only a reenactment of a book I once read. Joseph MacMoneagle, the best remote viewer in Stargate history, published a book of predictions in 1998, *The Ultimate Time Machine*. In it he recounts his remote views on various periods of time-space. One of his last predictions is about life in the distant future. He describes an earth exactly like the one I was seeing in my vision. Naturally, I wondered if I was somehow replaying that scene in my visit to the Arc.

The more I watched, the less my vision felt like a rehash and more like a new Living Video. A gift from the Generous One showing me feedback, follow-up on the effects of our work. Our precious transformational playground is safe and flourishing. We have saved it. We have brought the reality of the Infinite Abundance of Creation to earth. We have built a future of heaven on earth. We have done our jobs well. My whole being was filled with amazing excitement. The hairs were standing up on the back of my neck.

I don't often get a glimpse of the future. While directing a guided meditation for Quantum Selling before my stroke, I did see a massive earthquake stretching from Los Angeles to San Francisco. It was dark and rather upsetting. This vision of peace and hope was bright and clear, much more compelling and left me feeling … well, I guess it left me feeling satisfied and at peace.

I wanted to know more. Find out the year and date of this marvelous vision. See inside those domes. Watch the people go about their daily lives. Explore the business, the industry, all the mundane stuff that fosters personal curiosity, but really doesn't matter much to us in this time frame. I was thrilled beyond my wildest dreams to experience this vision. Thrilled, gratified and so very, very grateful. We had done it. We had done our part. The world was at peace. I could see our progeny thriving in the bounty of creation. But further exploration was not on my path.

I was drawn from this mesmerizing visage by the slightest of wind. The antithesis of that Category 5 hurricane we faced together. This was so small it couldn't even be called a breeze.

This barely noticeable wind was so tiny; in fact, it only affected the index finger on my right hand. You'll remember that was the finger that moved so slightly in the hospital. It was the finger whose tiny movement demonstrated to me the fulfillment of my promise of a full and complete recovery. That finger was the epicenter of the minuscule wind that drew me from my glimpse of the precious transformational playground to come. I was being given both a promise of our success and a vision of what that success looked like. It was a vision of the effect of the cause we created.

As I began to mentally focus more deeply on the slight wind, I hear the faintest buzzing sound. Focusing on this event, I feel the pressure of two very tiny feet perching on my prophetic finger. I managed to stay in Alpha as I open my eyes. I look down at the most remarkable sight. Perched on my index finger is the living Universal symbol of joy, happiness and peace. Sitting on my finger, wings flapping incredibly fast, is a tiny iridescent young hummingbird. An almost magical sense of divine power and awe surges though my body. He is telling me I can have anything I want. He is reminding me that all is well and I live in a world of Infinite Possibility. So powerful I can even have a hummingbird bring me a vision of peace and love. The feedback we need for our mission's success.

I watch as he flutters from my finger up to my face. He is so close to my face I felt the friction of his wings across my cheeks. He hovers in front of my eyes watching me for a long moment as if to say, "Are you getting this, Tom?"

Then he flies up into the trees and disappears.

It Only Takes A Moment

1. Think of all you wish to heal.
2. Hold a mental image of Tom assaulted by the Rainbow of Miracle Healing in the Presence of the Generous One.
3. Let your healing build strength, as the colors grow more and more vibrant.
4. Now, send your healing message as a blast of energy from your mind into the past and into another dimension.
5. Say: *Heal! Heal! Heal!*
6. Detach yourself completely from the outcome.
7. Embrace the rebound of the Miracle Healing you created.

You can do this. I know you can. You've done it before. I know. Because I saw you do it.

SPECIAL ONLINE BONUS

Quantum Healing Seminar

Quantum Selling is a proprietary system for reaching and selling millions from the comfort of your easy chair without using a computer or a phone in about the time it takes to drink a cup of coffee. Tom and Penelope developed and used this system very successfully to connect and sell advertising long before they introduced it to the general public. In fact, they refused to share it for ten years because it gave them such an advantage. Quantum Selling is based on the original US Army Stargate Program.

I'm telling you this so you'll understand the significance behind the Quantum Healing Seminar. While digging through old forgotten files I found a seminar titled *Quantum Masters/Healing Seminar*. Could this possibly relate to Generous One? I listened. I was shocked beyond words. Not only is it relevant, it's downright eerie.

We recorded this Quantum Healing Seminar March 19, 2009. Exactly nine days before my first death experience in the Arc of Light.

The Quantum Healing Seminar is yours free as a bonus for accepting the Gift I brought back for you from the Presence of the Generous One. We know this book will stir deep feelings within you, which you need time to process. The book stirs deep feelings because it is born in the Inscrutable Power of the Source of all Creation.

The Quantum Healing Seminar is a bit lighter and great for processing.

We hope you enjoy your experience. Register free at: https://www.richdreams.com/healingseminar

Good Luck and Great Adventures,
    Tom, Diane and Penelope Pauley

O! Join our Facebook Group Generous One for comments, discussion and Live presentations by author.

Made in the USA
Coppell, TX
14 December 2019